GOLDEN RETRIEVER TRAINING

All the tips you need for a well-trained Golden Retriever

By Mouss the Dog

AU PROGRAMME

FOREWORD...7

GOLDEN RETRIEVERS...9
- HISTORY 10
- TYPES OF GOLDEN RETRIEVERS................................. 10
- PHYSICAL SPECIFICITIES 11
- TEMPERAMENT 11
- GOLDEN RETRIEVERS: FOR WHOM? 12

UNDERSTANDING YOUR DOG...15
- UNDERSTANDING HIS BODY LANGUAGE 16
- UNDERSTANDING DOG LICKING 21
- WHY DO SOME DOGS DIG? 25
- WHY ARE THERE STEALING DOGS? 28
- WHY ARE THERE JEALOUS DOGS.............................. 30
- UNDERSTANDING DOG GROWLING 33
- PREVENTING DOG FIGHT.. 36
- HOW TO HAVE YOUR DOG AND CAT COHABITATE?.. 40

WHEN TO START HIS EDUCATION? ...45
- STARTING AS SOON AS POSSIBLE 46
- WHAT TO INSIST ON? 46

BASIC LEARNING...49
- LEARNING TO SIT 50
- LEARNING TO LIE DOWN 52
- LEARNING THE "STAY" COMMAND............................ 55
- LEARNING TO COME BACK 57

LEARNING TO WALK TO HEEL 60

SOCIALIZING...63

TEACHING CLEANLINESS 64

TEACHING NOT TO BARK 66

TEACHING NOT TO JUMP ON PEOPLE 70

LEARNING TO GO TO HIS BASKET 72

LEARNING TO STAY HOME ALONE 75

SOCIALIZING YOUR DOG 78

TEACHING TRICKS...83

TRAINING TO BRING BACK 84

TRAINING TO BOW 87

LEARNING TO SAY "HELLO" 90

GIVING A KISS 92

"TOUCH" TRAINING 94

TRAINING YOUR DOG TO "ROLL OVER" 96

LEARNING TO CRAWL 99

WALKING BACKWARDS 101

TURNING ON/OFF THE LIGHT 104

TRAINING TO RECOGNIZE ITEMS 106

TRAINING TO PUT HIS TOYS AWAY 109

TRAINING TO OPEN AND CLOSE DOORS 111

TRAINING TO PLAY DEAD 114

TRAINING TO SIT PRETTY 117

PLAYING WITH YOUR DOG...121

GAMES AND TRAINING 122

HOW MUCH TIME SHOULD BE GIVEN TO GAMES? 124

> DANGEROUS TOYS FOR YOUR DOG 126
>
> HOW TO CHOOSE THE PROPER TOYS? 129
>
> HIDE-AND-SEEK 132
>
> EDUCATING CHILDREN 135

DOG SPORTS...139

> INFORMATION ABOUT DOG AGILITY 140
>
> INFORMATION ABOUT FLYBALL 142
>
> INFORMATION ABOUT DOG SCOOTER 144
>
> INFORMATION ABOUT DOG JUMPING 147
>
> INFORMATION ABOUT CANICROSS... 149
>
> INFORMATION ABOUT HEELWORK TO MUSIC 151

TO CONTINUE...155

FOREWORD

First of all, we would like to thank you for choosing our book to start, or keep on, educating your Golden Retriever.

We intend to give you an overall view of the behavior to adopt with your dog and more importantly to identify the traps to avoid.

To make sure you get the keys to a harmonious relationship with your dog, we will guide you step by step through different thematics that will help you get closer to your companion. Keep in mind that this complicity is what will let you have a physically and mentally balanced dog which will make his education much easier.

We will start by telling you more about Golden Retrievers and then we will deal with several points in depth: dog behavior, basic training, socializing, learning tricks, games to play with him and canines sports.

We hope to give you lots of ideas to have as many activities as possible to bond with your Golden Retriever.

Don't hesitate to glance over the topics you already master and to take more time to study the new or difficult ones.

Use it as a textbook, picking daily the practical information you need.

Keep it by your side: you might need it soon!

Enjoy reading!

Mouss the Dog's team

GOLDEN RETRIEVERS

Golden Retrievers are probably the best illustration of what is "Man's best friend"!

We tend to forget that before being domestic dogs, Golden Retrievers used to be hounds.

Among the most popular dog breeds, they deserve their reputation of perfect pet, both nice and loving.

HISTORY

Finding the exact origin of the Golden Retriever is pretty difficult.

Like any other retriever dog, the Golden was at first used in hunting. This English breed originated in 1868, when Lord Tewdmonth crossbred a Wavy Coated male and a Tweed Water Spaniel female.

Other dog breeds are thought to have taken part in the process of creating the Golden breed, like the Saint-John's and the Irish Setter.

The Golden Retriever was first granted breed status in 1913 and got his final name in 1920.

Golden Retrievers have known an endless success since 1980 and are now considered as one of the favorite family dogs.

TYPES OF GOLDEN RETRIEVERS

Unlike Labradors, Golden Retrievers cannot be black. Therefore there is only one variety of Golden Retrievers even if they can vary from cream to dark golden, which are the only officially recognized colors. At first, Golden Retrievers were of an almost brown dark golden coat.

The clearer (white) or darker tones (mahogany, chocolate and black) are not registered as Golden Retriever's standards.

PHYSICAL SPECIFICITIES

Golden Retrievers are athletic dogs whose physical appearance is often compared to a Labrador Retriever. They are strong, sturdy and well-shaped dogs. Soft and fluffy, the Golden is also a strong dog.

The long tail does not curl up but has a nicely developed fringe that underlines the general figure.

The head, as well as the whole body, is well-proportioned. The falling ears frame a strong and large muzzle.

The dark brown eyes convey intelligence and benevolence through a gentle and nice look.

- **Weight**: ideally 75 pounds (34 kilos).
- **Height**: around 24 inches (61 cm).
- **Coat**: thick and half-long, falling into a fringe.

TEMPERAMENT

Golden Retrievers are gentle and sensitive dogs who need lots of love and affection. Great with kids, this breed fits in any family and will soon become a full member of your tribe!

As they do not like being alone, Golden Retrievers require a lot of attention and will prove to be a very present pet. As a consequence, they are also naturally friendly and loyal.

The Golden Retriever's intelligence and training capacities are not to be proved anymore. A well-trained Golden will be delighted to help his family. But make sure you do not push him around: he may react badly to reprimands and become stubborn when feeling forced into doing something.

This sporty breed enjoys going out and running; also, they feel more comfortable in wide-open spaces. Do not forget that Labradors have a hunter's instinct and will therefore need to discover the world. You'd better be ready for long walks!

GOLDEN RETRIEVERS: FOR WHOM?

Just like any other Retriever, the Golden needs space. He enjoys running as much as swimming and will therefore feel better in the countryside than in a city. It is clearly not an apartment pet.

Being a very loyal and friendly pet, he will be ideal for someone in search of a true companion. But make sure you keep in mind that your dog will need a lot of time at the risk of feeling abandoned if you do not care enough.

In return, you will be the proud owner of a loyal and always helpful dog. He will be a great companion for games and for life!

UNDERSTANDING YOUR DOG

UNDERSTANDING HIS BODY LANGUAGE

Eventhough he does not speak, your dog expresses himself. How can you understand his canine body language?

You almost expect him to speak, don't you? Maybe you are the one not knowing how to interpret what they say! Dogs use their whole body to communicate: eyes, back, tail, legs, lips... and more! This is called body language and we are going to give you the keys to understanding it!

UNDERSTANDING POSITIVE EMOTIONS THROUGH DOG BODY LANGUAGE

When he is happy or wants to share something positive with you, your dog is relaxed; his muscles are slack and loose. Differences can be observed depending on the specific emotion he is feeling.

WELL-BEING AND HAPPINESS
When he lies on his back, rubbing his shoulders, his loin and sometimes his muzzle on the ground, your dog shows his well-being. Isn't it delightfull to see him behaving this way? Half-shut eyes also express great satisfaction.

PLAYFUL
When he leans down in the sphinx position while his rear end stays up, your dog wants you to understand that he feels like playing and needs to unwind. This position often comes along with a smiling expression, mouth half-open. Some dogs also jump and yip.

FRIENDLY
Looking at you with his head slightly tilted is a friendly posture. In that case his body is usually curved and he sometimes wriggles his rear end. Some hands licking may also happen!

DELIGHT
When he is happy to see you or to go out for a walk your dog tries to express his enjoyment. Jumping on you, energetically moving his rear end and his tail, bowing, yipping, barking and sometimes moaning are so many manifestations of his delight.

FOCUSING
A dog can focus on your voice, on familiar or unknown noises and smells, even when you cannot perceive them. In this situation he pricks up his ears and holds his head up. He stays still with his eyes wide open. As long as he is not leaning forward on tense forelegs he is not worried, only on alert and focusing on something.

LOOKING FOR STROKES
A dog showing you his wriggling rear end is looking for strokes on his lower back. If he was looking for you to pat his belly, he would lie on his back, paws folded before him and chest exposed.

UNDERSTANDING NEGATIVE EMOTIONS THROUGH DOG BODY LANGUAGE

Because life is hardly a bed of roses for dogs either!

WARY DOG
When he perceives signals he finds worrying, the dog gets on alert: he bends forward with his neck stretched to the maximum, standing still. He may growl slightly.

FRIGHTENED OR WORRIED
Ears folded back and tail lowered, the dog arches his back and leans down a little. You can notice that the muscles are tense and the posture freezes. The dog may then growl and bark to show he is not comfortable. He may also yawn excessively to show his fright.

AGRESSIVE AND THREATENING

Aggressiveness can be caused by fear or by the need to get out of a frightening situation or the need to threaten and chase the odd one out.

To look intimidating, he has his hackles raised, stands straight and keeps his tail in line with spine. He shows his canines, his mouth half-open. He growls louder and louder and barks loudly. He stares but one should not look back at him for it would be understood as a sign of defiance and an invitation to attack. His tail flaps the floor slowly but strongly.

Most of the time, these signals are warnings: it is still possible to neutralize the attack although it is imminent.

If this situation happens with your own dog, you should not defy him nor submit yourself. In case it is not your dog you should adopt a submissive posture. In any case, abrupt gestures are to be avoided.

NERVOUS DOG

There is no general rule to identify a nervous dog's reaction when he is not in a fighting situation. He can scratch or lick insistently a specific part of his body or give an enormous yawn several times in a row.

IMPORTANT MESSAGES IN DOG BODY LANGUAGE

In a dog's life, and depending on the context, there are variations other than emotions. For instance, hierarchy is known to be very important to them.

SUBMISSION AND DOMINATION

The submissive dog tries to look smaller than he is. For example he can lie on his back or curl up. Looking away, his tail low and his hackles raised, he lowers his neck while his muzzle looks up at the dominant one. He will sometimes sniff him and give him a lick to calm the situation down and show he is not competing.

On the other hand, the dominant dog intends to look bigger than he is by arching his back. He leans forward, ears up or slightly forward. His tail remains in line with his spine while he growls with his mouth shut, staring at his competitor. This is an aggressive domination behavior.

Putting one leg on the other dog, overlapping or sexual simulation are so many signals of a pacific domination.

AFFECTION AND PACIFICATION

After going through a difficult situation, a dog usually yawns. For example when you see your dog yawning while you are scowling him, it does not mean he does not care or gets bored: he is just trying to calm the situation down! When he nuzzles or licks your face, he wants to show how much he cares for you.

NEEDING SOMETHING AND HUNGRY

Every dog has his own way of asking for something or begging for food. Some shake hands while others bark, moan or nuzzle your arms and legs. The owner needs to take this behavior into account but without giving an immediate response for it would make the dog believe he is in command.

BOREDOM AND LACK OF ATTENTION

A bored dog may yawn, scratch the floor, indefinitely lick an object, sit on your way in the sphinx position staring at you; he can also insist on shaking hands.

SOCIALIZING

Remember that the anal glands are a sort of identity card for dogs. By sniffing one another, they learn a lot about their fellow dogs' sex, age and health. They may behave the same way with humans, especially when they are still puppies. Although we do not have these very informative glands they manage to learn a lot by sniffing us.

THE LIMITS OF ANTHROPOMORPHISM

We should not consider that a dog is a four-legged copy of humans. His reactions are not imitations of ours and many owner/dog relationships suffer because the owner misinterpreted the signals.

For example, putting his leg on a human's arm or lap is not a dog's friendly gesture but a domination act. The dog is being frank and clear; therefore he will not understand your reactions if they do not match his warnings. Remember to always remain an observer and not to transfer your emotions on his. A dog does not take his revenge on you by breaking stuff while you are away; he feels abandoned and this anxiety makes him unwind on objects.

UNDERSTANDING DOG LICKING

Your dog does not know how to hold his tongue? And you are tired of finding it on your feet?

As humans do not act the same way, you sometimes wonder how to interpret this behavior. The intended message actually depends on the situation and on the object the dog is licking. Mouss is going to help you break a code as old as time: body language!

LICKING BETWEEN PUPPIES AND THEIR MOTHER

From the very start of their lives, puppies get used to licking: it is the way their mother reassures them, cleans them or demonstrates her affection.

After they are weaned, the puppies develop the reflex of licking their mother's nose to tell her they are hungry. In the world of domestic dogs this is only a signal whereas wolves use it as a stimulation to regurgitate half-digested food which is highly indigestible for their under development stomach.

Some dogs will need time to break the habit of licking their owner's hands when they would love to have a bite… to eat.

DOGS LICKING ONE ANOTHER

As far as we can tell, licking has always been a very significant reflex between wolves or dogs. When meeting an unknown dog he considers as dominant, aggressive or dangerous, your dog will calm the situation down by licking him. This is the way your dog says: "I'm not looking for a fight with you, we are friends and everything is okay between us!"

In this case, licking is both a peaceful social behavior and a sign of submission. By refusing a fight, the licking dog shows the other one that he accepts to be considered as hierarchically inferior.

When two dogs know and appreciate each other, mutual licking is just a display of affection, the way we kiss or hug.

WHY DO DOGS LICK HUMANS?

The reasons why a dog licks humans come more or less directly from his ancestral reflexes. The dog licks his owner to tell him that:

- He recognizes him as hierarchically superior (submission).
- He loves him and is happy to see him and spend time together (affection).
- He is hungry. That's the signal he would use with his mummy!

Your dog may also lick you because:

- He likes the salted taste of your sweat after sports. In this case he will insistently lick your face, neck, arms, and feet.
- He likes the smell of your shower gel or moisturizer.
- He is trying to identify your mood and looking for the pheromones that would help him out. In this case, he focuses on your hands and feet.
- During an examination, your dog will lick the vet to ask for good care and no pain (he is slightly worried).
- Very scarcely, the dog will insistently lick one of his owners because he mistakes him for a sexual partner. To avoid his becoming possessive and jealous you need to put him back in his place as soon as possible.

Once he is done licking, and whichever the reason for it, always remember to conscientiously wash the zones he has licked: your immune system is not the same as his and the risk of catching an infection is real.

COMPULSIVE LICKING

A random behavior can become compulsive when it occupies too much time and thoughts. Licking is a normal act for a dog but licking endlessly the same object reveals a problem.

WHY DOES A DOG LICK HIMSELF?

The first reason for a dog to lick his body is also the most evident one: hygiene. In that case, he licks himself quickly and then stops.

You should pay attention to his behavior when he starts licking a specific part of his body with insistence. This behavior can mean that:

- He is stressed. Licking is an OCD (obsessive-compulsive disorder) that relaxes him but insisting on a specific zone (leg or groin) might brush his hairs away, irritate his skin or even wound him. A vet or a behaviorist will help you with stopping this behavior.
- He is hurt and tries to ease the pain. Identify the licked zone and inform your vet about it.

WHY DOES MY DOG LICK OBJECTS?

A dog may carefully lick the floor, a chair, a toy, a cushion or else. This is only his way of giving an exploring taste to a new environment. Nothing to worry about!

A dog quietly licking a toy while sitting in his basket or on a carpet might be bored. In this case you just need to take him out for a walk or have him play to change his mind.

If this behavior becomes compulsive, it might signal OCD. In this situation, try to figure out the context that triggers this licking to identify the cause of stress. Again, do not hesitate to ask for professional help.

WHY DO SOME DOGS DIG?

The earth is full of smells. This is why digging is a pleasure for dogs! And it is also their way of rebinding with their ancestors: they have been digging from father to son for millenaries! Nevertheless, this strange behavior sometimes upsets humans. Some of them have even found ways to make dogs loose this habit.

THE REASONS WHY DOGS DIG

Digging the ground is a natural activity for dogs, it is an ordinary behavior.

Here are the main reasons why:

- ◯ **Boredom**: After being alone in the garden for 15 minutes without any stimulation, the dog may get bored. He digs to unwind a little.
- ◯ **Heat**: When feeling warm, the dog starts digging to find a shelter into the fresh ground.
- ◯ **Burying**: He is making his own stock of food! Saving some biscuits or bones is an ancestral reassuring technics for dogs in fear of starving.
- ◯ **Playing**: With twigs or buried roots.
- ◯ **Searching**: He smelt something attractive: small rodents in their lair, small animals' carcasses, cats' droppings, insect's larva...
- ◯ **To leave home**: If he is digging close to the limit of your garden and towards the outside, look at what is around: dogs, kids, animals... Maybe your doggy only needs to socialize more.

HOW TO REACT WHEN YOUR DOG IS DIGGING?

If seeing your dog conscientiously destroying your plantations and lawn makes you lose your temper... you are going to have to deal with it!

You cannot punish a dog for behaving "naturally". He will never understand it, especially if the digging happened several hours earlier.

If you catch the dog red-handed, you can say "No!" and take him somewhere else to distract him with another activity: play with a ball, make exercises, learn new tricks, play with you.

Avoid immediately taking him out for a walk: he will think it is the reward for having dug well. And you do not want him to try and please you by digging more!

TIPS TO STOP YOUR DOG FROM DIGGING

Don't worry: there are many ways of keeping your dog's mind away from your flowerbeds.

When he is alone in the garden for a few minutes, give him his favorite toys so he can have fun.

When the weather is hot, consider a swimming-pool, a cooling mat or a shadowy area.

Take him for longer walks in new places. He will get an opportunity to unwind, satisfy his curiosity and – who knows? – maybe even dig in the middle of nature!

Protect the places you don't want him to dig by adding wire mesh or twigs on the floor, citrus fruits peel near your plants, big rocks on the already dug holes: this should discourage him.

If your dog keeps on digging you will need to lure him into a compromise: define a specific area for him to dig. To have him forget that the rest of your garden even exists, melt the earth of his allowed digging area with sand and burry bones, treats, *kongs* (a toy filled with dog biscuits): in a word, priceless surprises!

There is no need to say that you should be very careful and bury them at a time your dog can not see you! Same thing for gardening: avoid digging the earth in front of your dog: he might want to impress you by mimicking you!

WHY ARE THERE STEALING DOGS?

This is a mind disposition: some dogs steal, others don't. Food, shoes, your baby's toys... Life can quickly get complicated if your dog takes this bad habit. You'd better react quickly and educated him not to touch your belongings.

THE RISKS

For your dog, everything is either a game or food. Things you find disgusting like a roting dead animal, a plastic bag, a torn tire, are very attractive objects to him. Most of the time, his stomach deals very well with this diet. But there can be accidents.

Moreover, if your dog gets used to helping himself into your things, on your table or in your garbage, he can react agressively because he does not understand your reaction the day you decide he has gone too far. This opens the door to all sorts of crises!

Finally, and there is probably no need to draw you a picture, the stealing dog helps himself into your plate and bowls which are to be taken immediately to the dishwasher. He can also hide the stolen objects which can become an unbearable attitude if you have to spend your time looking for everything.

TRAPS TO AVOID

Your dog steals because he does not make the difference between his things and yours. If you scoll him he won't do it again... in your presence. You are going to face trust issues at home!

Never give food to your dog from your own plate: the smallest treat and he will consider that your food can also be his. Generally speaking if you are used to giving him the leftovers, the best is to pour it into his bowl while he is not watching. Until your dog gets used to it, do not leave any temptation under his nose!

Some owners laugh when their dog catches an object and takes it away. This reaction will only comfort the dog in the idea that you are playing some kind of game. All the more if you then follow him to try and catch the object. He will either enjoy it a lot or get angry and bite.

HOW TO EDUCATE A STEALING DOG?

As usual, you should not overreact nor ignore the situation. When the dog gets close to the food, you should order him a strong « No » and repeat it as many times as necessary. When he seems to understand that your food is not for him, reward him with one of his own biscuits.

If the dog has been stealing objects, take advantage of his being away to take them back and put them back in their place. You can even associate the place where they belong to something unpleasant: a pile of cartboard ready to fall over the shoes or the lid ready to fall on the bin. It will have the double advantage of making him flee and of warning you.

Consider also that you dog will be less tempted to steal your stuff if he has his own. Having his toys always and immediately available will make stealing the others' less interesting!

WHY ARE THERE JEALOUS DOGS

A dog can absolutely feel jealous! This feeling can be triggered by the arrival of someone new into the house. This is why a dog and a baby frequently don't get along in the first weeks. In this case it is very important to think well ahead about your dog's education because a small jealousy may quickly lead to real relationship issues. Let's see how you should react when your dog is acting jealous.

MY DOG IS JEALOUS: IS IT NORMAL?

Not long ago our neighbors became happy parents. The problem is that Kitty, their Chihuahua, did not enjoy the experience at all. She started looking for their attention by barking or yipping as soon as they were taking care of their baby.

This apparition of jealousy between a dog and a baby is very frequent. The reason is that a dog's behavior is made of small habits. If something upsets these habits, like a new pet, a child or a new boyfriend or girlfriend, a dog can easily become jealous...

Actually, dog's jealousy is not a natural phenomenon. It is often triggered by a change in an owner's overprotective behavior.

Our neighbor was used to staying with Kitty all the time, pampering her and permanently taking care of her. She even calls her "baby". But now that there is another baby in the house, her dog is jealous. And that is only because Kitty does not receive the same attention as she used to.

HOW TO REACT WHEN FACING DOG JEALOUSY?

To prevent a dog from becoming jealous, the best is to think ahead about his education, from his very childhood. The biggest mistake when educating your dog is to consider him as a child or a human. The first step is to understand his behavior.

If it is already too late and your dog is jealous, you have to follow a series of steps:

DISCOVER WHERE THE JEALOUSY COMES FROM
Jealousy is caused by change. Start by clearly identifying what upsets your pet the most. A dog can become jealous because you do not give him enough attention anymore, or because you give his toys to another pet.

GET YOUR DOG USED TO A NEW SITUATION
In the event of the arrival of a baby or of a new pet in the house, your jealous dog will need reassurance. The worst you could do is to lock him up and not care about him anymore. Find a way for your dog to progressively get used to this arrival so that the newcomer is not perceived as traumatizing.

CHANGE THE DOG'S BEHAVIOR
Jealousy is a behavior problem. To have your pet change his behavior, you have to educate him and teach him new ways.

Reward him for being calm in the presence of the cause of his jealousy and have him understand the behavior you expect from him. If necessary, ignore your dog when he adopts the bad behavior. But beware of completely putting him aside: his jealousy might worsen!

DO NOT BE AGGRESSIVE
Never react negatively to the dog's jealousy. Remember that you are both responsible for this situation. Being aggressive might push your dog into behaving the same.

When a dog's jealousy becomes too invasive and you can not stop him at all, it is important to react. The best is to ask for a canine behaviorist's help: he will be perfectly able to help you out.

UNDERSTANDING DOG GROWLING

Irritated? In a bad mood? Nervous? Even humans sometimes growl on the people around! Your dog can feel overtaken by events too. As worrying as this behavior can be, the response should be adapted in order to avoid misdemeanors and misunderstandings. Better than getting into a fight, here is what you can do to put smiles back on everyone's face!

WHY DOES YOUR DOG GROWL?

Growling is associated with aggressiveness but we often misinterpret its meaning. A growl does not imply an imminent bite but it is part of a normal communication process and does not mean your dog has a problem.

The dog's growl is a response to a stressful situation. Growling is a warning that intends to avoid conflict.

It has several possible causes: fear, pain, stress, defense…

In dogs' communication code, it is a very clear signal of discomfort and it aims at avoiding an argument. In dogs' language, growling means: "you are bothering me, leave me alone!" or "I'm scared, get away from me!"

The problem is that people take it for a rebellious attitude and fear an imminent bite. So they usually respond with an act of violent punition. This reaction is absolutely not understandable for the dog who was precisely providing information to avoid this situation.

WHAT SHOULD YOU DO WHEN YOUR DOG GROWLS?

Beware: these explanations do not mean that you have to let your dog growl every time he is annoyed by something. The situation would get unbearable and neither of you would be happier this way.

Whenever your dog growls on you or someone close to you, it means he feels overtaken, worried or disturbed by an element of the situation. According to their own story, dogs are sensitive to different elements.

Here are some advices on how to react when your dog growls:

- ◯ **Make the distressing situation stop:** a loud noise, another dog's presence, hugs, a game. Any of these is an acceptable response for the dog who should stop growling.
- ◯ **Try to identify the trigger of the growling**: pain, stress, discomfort, fear…
- ◯ **In case of frequent growling**, take your dog to the vet or to a behaviorist to bring the harmony back between your dog and yourself.
- ◯ **In the good times**, pat him and reward him to strengthen your relationship.

Sometimes, teaching a command as if it were a reward is enough to calm the atmosphere and to bring back good relationships.

TRAPS TO AVOID

Your dog expects a pacific reaction to his growling so do not:

- ◯ **Look at a growling dog in the eyes:** it is a sign of challenge. It will be understood as a provocation.
- ◯ **Corner a frightened dog**: he growls to say he wants to flee because he is scared so if he feels trapped, he may bite to escape the situation.
- ◯ **Insist in the disturbing attitude** thinking that will get the dog used to it and tame him. On the contrary, this will increase his discomfort and therefore his aggressiveness.

- ○ **Think that the dog is growling to dominate you.** This is false: he growls to give a message. If you do not try to understand him but respond violently, you may deeply deteriorate the bounds between you two.
- ○ **Think your dog is crazy** and does not like you. Some owners abandon a growling dog because they think he is violent and insensitive. This is a complete misunderstanding: growling is an expression of the dog's sensitivity to a situation.

PREVENTING DOG FIGHT

Dogs love squaberring, especially males! But a basic fighting game happens to become a real dog fight. The situation becomes dangerous for the dogs and their owners. This is why you should always avoid dog fight.

UNDERSTANDING THE MOTIVE OF A DOG FIGHT

Just like humans, dogs have an inherent part of aggressiveness. The reason is that dogs have the instinct of a pack animal and they determine their position amongst the pack by hierarchical confrontations. Fighting is part of their identity.

However, a dog fight should never be left to worsen for an aggressive behavior may lead to many accidents and endanger the health of the dog, of his owner or of the people close by.

THE CAUSES OF A DOG FIGHT

It is always difficult to understand the reason why two dogs quarrel. That is probably because there are as many fights as reasons for dogs to fight.

Among the most common reasons, we can find:

- **Hierarchy**: dogs try to show one another "who is the boss".
- **Territorial invasion**: an aggressive dog will try and defend his territory against the intruder.
- **Fear**: a fearful dog attacks because he feels cornered.
- **Competition**: two dogs can fight over a bone or a treat.
- **Aggressiveness**: having developed a bad behavior will make the dog fight against any other dog.

HOW TO RECOGNIZE AN AGRESSIVE BEHAVIOR?

Understanding the reason why dogs fight may not be very important. Yet, it will become important if your pet regularly attacks other dogs. You will then have to try and explain the aggressive behavior of the dog and cure it.

In that purpose, the best is to call on a dog behaviorist: he is the only one who can understand the reasons why your dog attacks.

HOW TO REACT WHEN FACING A DOG FIGHT?

It is primordial to make the fight stop as soon as possible because two aggressive dogs will eventually end up fighting. And no one really wants a dog fight to come to an end. Not reacting might lead to much worse problems.

Here are some advices to prevent or stop a dog fight:

RECOGNIZING A SITUATION OF FIGHT

Sometimes, basic fighting games between dogs worsen to real fights. To prevent this, always keep an eye on your pet when he is playing with another dog. In case of excessive growling, bites or yipping, separate the dogs before the fight starts. Generally speaking, avoid letting your dog play with an unknown dog.

NEVER PHYSICALLY INTERFERE IN A DOG FIGHT

In case the fight already started, do not throw yourself into it. You might get bitten, even by your own dog. Do not try to grab the dog's collar with unprotected hands. This would be way too dangerous for you. Using a large object (like a stick) to separate the animals is a good option.

USE A BUCKET OF WATER

A safer solution to have the fight stop is to throw water at the dogs. This will calm them down instantly and they will naturally separate. Then, you can take the dogs away from one another.

USE LOUD NOISES

Any other way of getting the dogs' attention can make the fight stop. For instance, you can try using a high pitched whistle or you can bang on saucepans. If you manage to get their attention, it will be easier to separate them.

If two dogs have already been in a fight, you must prevent them from having any contact. They might fight again as soon as they get a chance!

AGRESSIVE DOG: WHAT SHOULD I DO?

If your pet is causing many fights, it is essential that you try anything you can to avoid a new quarrel. An aggressive dog can bring many troubles to his owner.

For example, if your dog hurts someone, you will be considered as fully responsible. Your dog could also be hurt in a fight or worse: you may have to have him put down by a vet.

To avoid your dog's aggressive behavior to have a tragic ending, you may want to follow these advises:

- **Always keep him on the leash**: first of all, an aggressive dog should never be let alone in a public place. Make sure that you are always in control of your dog: the leash should be resistant and adapted to your dog.
- **Limit walks in public places**: if your dog's behavior becomes unbearable whenever he meets other pets, avoid taking him to crowded places.

- **Buy a muzzle** to prevent your dog from biting other dogs or walkers by.
- **Consulte a behaviorist**: last but not least, trying to treat the aggressive behavior of the dog is the best way to deal with it. In that case, you may need to consult a dog behaviorist: he will help you understand and control your pet.

HOW TO HAVE YOUR DOG AND CAT COHABITATE?

Your home atmosphere got colder after a new protégé entered the family? For the dog as well as for the cat, accepting a newcomer is a more or less difficult challenge. It does not depend on you that they become best friends but it is your responsibility to prevent war and – don't worry – it is possible! Let's try and understand what is at stake and examine the basic rules from all angles.

WHY IS IT HARD FOR CATS AND DOGS TO GET ALONG?

This is a long story! These two species are not naturally supposed to cohabitate. Cats have the ancestral memory of the dog being their predator. A dog trying to play with him can look like a threat to the cat. On the other hand, the dogs do not understand the individualist and independent behavior of the cat. In one word: they both have preconceptions about the other.

Moreover, their communication codes are very different which leads to misunderstandings.

The cat wags his tail when he feels hostile and anoyed. The dog wags his tail to show his enthusiasm and when he wants to play. For the dog, a cat waging his tail is inviting him to play! Here is for the misunderstanding...

THE RISKS OF A TROUBLED COHABITATION

It is important to make sure the relation between them is at least indifferent because a conflict would make victims.

The cat or the dog can develop an obsession over the other one and make his life a living hell: no access to his bowl, to the litter, to his crate, blows, bites, scratches... Cats have been seen in a bad shape after being harassed by a dog; and the other way round...

You probably do not want your home to become a torture center for one of your two companions, especially as the torturer will not be much happier than his victim.

Not mentioning the risks of fights that would have consequences on your home organization.

THE IDEAL MEETING FOR A HAPPY DOG/CAT COHABITATION

Childhood is known to be the most malleable moment of life for every species. Puppies and kittens are no exception to this rule. It is much easier to create good relationships when at least one of them is still a baby. The animal is going through his socialization phase until his 12th week for the dog and his 9th for the cat, which means he becomes easily attached to any being living around him. Therefore this is the perfect moment to forge a lifelong friendship with a pet from another species.

The presence of a baby is perceived by an adult cat or dog as a disturbance but not as a threat. The stress remains lower and even if some yowling and barking are heard at the beginning, they will not stop them from observing and getting to know each other. Games can also help these first moments along.

SOLUTIONS TO MAKE THE DOG/CAT COHABITATION EASIER

Obviously, it is not always possible to have them meet when they are babies. If they are both adults, the battle is not lost but you will have to follow some rules.

GESTURES THAT HELP DOG AND CAT KNOW EACH OTHER

Your gentle presence is required on their first meeting.

- Let them know each other's smell through a door during one day or two before they find themselves face to face.
- Separate their bowls: the cat will feel safer if his food is on top of a shelf, out of the dog's reach.
- The cat needs an escape option, like a piece of furniture to jump on.
- It is the cat's pace that will be followed: he might need an observation time before he goes to meet the dog.
- If the dog knows the "do not touch" command, it is even better: the cat will appreciate not being forced to contact! It is important that you keep the dog's behavior under control to prevent him from being invasive. If you believe he is too excited, it may be good to isolate him until he calms down before renewing the experiment.

TRAPS TO AVOID

- One can be tempted to reassure and cuddle the newcomer more than the "old one". Pets are observant and sensible to injustice; this behavior will do no good to the newcomer. It is important when both pets are here to remain fair as to cuddles, attentions, love words and treats.
- Impose a contact to the cat will only antagonize him. Let him get used to the situation at his own pace until he feels ready.

At last, never hesitate to ask for a behaviorist to neutralize a crisis before it is too late. Sometimes, you only need a small change to make life easier!

WHEN TO START HIS EDUCATION?

As many other owners before, you will quickly succumb to your puppy's charm. But this is no excuse for not educating him. As the dog's behavior is built during the first months of his life, it is very important to educate a puppy if you do not want him to become a little monster.

It is especially true for large dog breeds that may become more and more invasive if they are not well educated. But it is also true for small dog breeds.

STARTING AS SOON AS POSSIBLE

As the dog's behavior is modeled during his youth, you will have to start educating him as soon as he enters your home, meaning when he is 2 months old. Dogs need to be taken on since their earliest childhood.

It is important to have him understand very early what he can and can not do. But do not be mean to him: puppies are always playful and it is normal for them to do stupid things... The best is to show them step by step what they have to do by choosing treats over punishment.

WHAT TO INSIST ON?

When they are young they learn fast... but still, they need some time! Be tolerant with a boisterous puppy: it is normal for a young dog to share his *joie de vivre*.

However, never compromise when it comes to hierarchy. They have to understand who the master is when they are young. This is the moment they "analyze" the members of the family and determine who is the most important, to whom he should obey or who can be subjected. If you let your puppy rule, he will feel on top of hierarchy and you can be sure he will be an uncontrollable adult.

BASIC LEARNING

LEARNING TO SIT

"Sit" is the one command every dog owner should teach. Properly training a dog will eventually include this position, useful in many circumstances.

Having your dog sit on command is a very good start in a puppy's training. Teaching the "sit" command to a dog is pretty easy because it is a natural position.

Here is the method:

1. **Use a reward**: first of all you need to find a treat your dog likes: a dog biscuit or anything he likes. Avoid chocolate and sugar which are poisonous to dogs.
2. **Squat down near your dog**: at first, do not give any signal or order to him. Just get close to him with his treat in your hand.
3. **Make your dog sit**: to make him sit, you only need to put your hand holding the treat closer to him. Slowly raise your hand until it is over his head but always keeping a safe distance from his mouth. Your dog will naturally sit to keep his eyes fixed on his treat.
4. **Congratulate your dog**: once he is sitting, you only have to give him his treat and congratulate him, repeating out loud the word "sit" so that he will eventually associate it to this position.

Of course, properly training a dog implies repetition. You will have to do this exercise several times for your dog to learn the sitting position.

To avoid his associating obedience and treat, make sure the treat is smaller each time until you do not give him anything anymore.

The most important is that you keep on congratulating and stroking your dog at the end of this exercise. Eventually he will not need any treat to obey when you command him to sit.

LEARNING TO LIE DOWN

Dogs love learning new tricks, even as puppies. It is an opportunity for them to develop their intelligence (and to get treats!) and a chance for you to spend good time together. One basic and useful trick is to teach your dog to lie down on command.

WHY SHOULD HE LEARN HOW TO LIE DOWN?

Finding the ideal position when you have to stay still is not easier for dogs than it is for humans. If you are waiting somewhere and it might take some time, your dog will get tired whether he sits or stands. Why not showing him the best position right away?

Moreover, when he is lying down, your dog is much quieter. Asking him to lie down is a better way than getting angry or yelling at him when you want him to calm down, for example after a great game session.

Be careful not to order your dog to lie down when you send him to his basket or punish him for misbehaving otherwise he will confuse order with punishment. He would feel punished every time you ask him to lie down even though he did not do anything bad.

In any case your dog must already know the "sit" command to learn the "lie down".

TRADITIONNAL TECHNIQUE TO LEARN HOW TO LIE DOWN

This one is easy: you just need to wait for your dog to be sited.

- You face him and nicely hold his forelegs and pull them towards you.

- The dog will automatically find himself lying down. While doing this, repeat "lie down" so that he associates the words with the position.
- Once he is lying down, you can stroke him and congratulate him.

You will of course have to repeat it many times: 5 to 10 times a day during several weeks.

If your dog resists or complains, stop and look for what is bothering him. Maybe the floor is unpleasant, maybe he is preoccupied by an external element or maybe your gestures are too quick.

In any case do not force him, do not pull his legs against his will and do not push his back to force it to the ground.

POSITIVE TECHNIQUES TO LEARN HOW TO LIE DOWN

Nowadays, positive techniques are often chosen over others. They involve bringing the dog to understanding an order and to executing it willingly using rewards.

USING A TREAT
- When your dog is sitting, get his attention with a biscuit or a treat.
- When he tries to catch it, lower your hand to the ground and bring the biscuit to you until your dog is lying.
- Say "lie down" and give him the biscuit while congratulating him.
- Repeat several times.

After some time, add the gesture of showing the floor with your finger. Keep on ordering "lie down" and on giving him a treat when he obeys.

After 2 to 3 weeks, you can slowly stop giving him treats but keep on patting him.

USING A TOY

This technique is mostly used on puppies. In this case, the idea is to create a new rule to his favorite game.

- Be close to his basket and throw him a ball.
- When he brings it back, congratulate him and say "lie down" showing him the basket. This is the rule he has to follow to have you throw the ball again.

After a few days, once he has mastered this rule, he will start to go to his basket on demand.

This method is compatible with the previous one as it associates the basket to the command, which can be very useful if you want your dog to stay calm at home.

LEARNING THE "STAY" COMMAND

This is the most impressive command to teach a dog: it takes a very strong discipline to teach a puppy to stay still in any circumstances. But it is not impossible!

WHY SHOULD HE LEARN THE "STAY" COMMAND?

Teaching your dog not to move is a very useful trick. Having him stay still is a good way to control his energy and to show your hold on the animal.

This trick may also be very useful in everyday life: a dog who knows the "stay" command will be less tempted to run away or to escape as soon as the house door is open. It will also limit the risks of car accidents, frequents when a nervous dog refuses to stop.

THE TECHNIQUE TO TEACH THE "STAY" COMMAND TO A DOG

As always in dog training, teaching him not to move is a matter of patience and discipline. But it is not that difficult once you know how to proceed:

1. **Mastering the "sit" command**: the "stay" command will not be the first trick you teach your dog. A puppy's training will have to start with the basic "sit" command, also very useful. It is a necessary step your dog has to take before learning to stay still.

2. **The basics**: once your dog obeys the "sit" command, you will have to make this order slowly evolve into a "stay still" command. Start by commanding your dog to sit, then take a step away from him saying "stay" and making the gesture you want him to associate with this order

(showing the palm of your hand for instance). Reward him as soon as he stays still, even if only for a second. Start with practicing at home so that the outdoor noises do not distract him.

3. **The training**: training a dog is a matter of repetition and patience. When your dog starts to stay still on command when you take a step backward, you can take more steps. Be progressive: from one step to two, then three or four. Keep on quickly rewarding him (a few seconds after giving the command) because a non-trained dog will not stay still during 10 seconds. The more your dog obeys this command, the longer you wait to give him a treat.

4. **Turning your back at him**: once your dog obeys to the three-four steps away command, he needs to learn to stay still even if you break the visual contact. Start the exercise over again, turning slowly your back on him and walking away. A non-educated dog will follow you and you should control this attitude.

5. **Out of the room**: once your dog obeys when you turn your back on him you will have to keep on training to leave the room. You give the command but this time you completely walk away and leave the room so that your dog cannot see you anymore. At first, come back quickly and give your dog a treat.

6. **Outdoor**: once your dog knows how to stay still even if you get out of the room, try it outdoor. With the noises and agitation, a dog will be less focused at first. You will have to start the training over, step by step, until he becomes perfectly obedient.

LEARNING TO COME BACK

Calling your dog back to your feet is one of the most useful things when training a puppy: it is unconceivable to take a dog out without a leash if he does not know the "heel" (or "come here") command. Besides, teaching him this command is the best way to avoid accidents and to make his walks safer. Let's see how to train your dog to come back to your feet.

TRAPS TO AVOID

- **Not using a command**: training a dog goes through the use of a command. Therefore, you cannot call your dog back only by saying his name. Instead of calling his name, use a command like "[name of the dog], heels!"
- **Starting the training outdoor**: systematically trying to teach this command outdoor is another common mistake. Training a puppy is a step by step practice; it is better to start in a quiet place. Of course, the "come here" command will eventually take you to a park or an outdoor place but this should not be the first step.
- **Making the "heel" command a punishment**: another common mistake made by many owners is to use this command only to end a walk. They also get angry and chase the dog if he does not obey immediately. By acting this way, your dog might consider the "come here" command as a punishment that ends his games or walks. Make sure you include this command into a rewarding context and not systematically end a dog walk by a "come here" command. Do not put your dog on the leash right after commanding him to come to you. And when you put him on the leash, keep on walking for a while so he does not consider the "heel" command as the signal of the end of good times. Besides, always avoid getting angry while

teaching this command to a dog. It would be the best way to make him *not* come to your heel!

HOW TO TEACH IT PROPERLY?

Here is a step by step method to teach a dog the "heel" command. As for every step of your dog training, this one will need both your patience and time:

1) START AT HOME

Training a puppy starts as soon as he enters the house. To call your dog back, you will start practicing at home.

Start using this command on the first weeks so he gets used to it. For example: "[name of the dog], heel" or "[name of the dog], come here". You can also use a gesture for your dog to memorize.

When your puppy is away from you, use the "heel" command and congratulate him when he comes back to you. But this will obviously not be enough for him to learn it perfectly.

2) GO OUTSIDE

You will very quickly need to practice outside: without a big space, this command is useless. At first, it is better to choose a closed place where there is no traffic. The best is a fenced garden, yours or a friend's, so your dog cannot run away or get hurt by a car.

To teach the "come here" command, let your dog go away and then order him to come back. If he obeys, reward him with strokes and a treat. If he does not obey, repeat the command without raising your voice, making sure that he can see you and hear you. If your dog ignores you after several attempts, act as if you were leaving without looking at him. He will feel abandoned and therefore come to you.

Never yell or run after your dog. He might get scared or think you are playing. Repeat this exercise regularly until your dog comes back quasi automatically.

3) IN PUBLIC

The next step is to go to an open space, like a public park, where your pet will be in contact with other humans and pets.

You will use the exact same method (command "heel" or "come here" followed by a reward) but you will have to proceed when your pet is very far away or distracted by a game or by other pets.

At first, practice this command on a very regular basis, without putting him on the leash. Then, allow intervals between the commands and alternate the situations. Sometimes you can walk him on the leash then let him go, sometimes you can leave him walk freely and try to have him follow you, etc.

If your dog does not obey your command, pretend to be walking away until he catches you back. Do not punish a dog when he is at your heels: he would consider it better not to obey. On the contrary, use positive training by rewarding him. If your pet comes to you when asked, reward him. If he does not, ignore him and do not reward him when he is finally back.

LEARNING TO WALK TO HEEL

One of the first goals of a dog owner, when going out for a walk, is to master the walk to heel. Untrained puppies tend to let their enthusiasm rule and pull on the leash. You'd better know how to control it to avoid struggling during every walk.

WHY SHOULD YOU TRAIN YOUR DOG TO WALK TO HEEL?

Let's consider this bad example Mouss shares with us: "Titus, my neighbor's German Shepherd, is full of energy. He was never taught how to walk to heel and tends to be the one taking his owner out for a walk. Titus runs towards the other dogs he sees in the street and forces his owner to run along with him. What an embarrassment!"

If you do not want to be taken out for a walk by your dog, you'd better teach him to walk to heel. Even with a small breed dog, a walk can quickly become a real ordeal if the untrained dog never listens to anyone else.

Even worse, it can become dangerous: an untrained dog has more chances to be run over by a car if he slips out of your control.

Finally, training a dog to walk to heel is the first and necessary step to walking him off leash.

ADVICES TO SIMPLIFY THE TEACHING

Here are advices to teach your doggy how to walk to heel:

- ○ Avoid going to the same places every time so your dog understands you are the one deciding on the itinerary.
- ○ Use a long and flexible leash so your dog is not tempted to pull on it.

- When your dog pulls towards a specific direction, go the opposite way so he understands he is not the one taking decisions.
- Always walk on a quiet pace to avoid your dog feeling nervous and to make him naturally follow you.
- Adjust your walk to be the exact opposite of what your dog wants: if he gets faster, slow down and if he slows down, walk faster. You must be the only one deciding on the pace.
- If your puppy tries to overtake you, stop and make him come back to you so he understands that you are the only one taking decisions.

SOCIALIZING

TEACHING CLEANLINESS

Cleanliness is one of the first lessons to give to your puppy, mostly because there is nothing more upsetting than having a dog doing his business in your house. The first weeks will be very important in the cleanliness training process. But it happens that an already well-trained dog starts peeing in the house. In that case, your dog might have a problem. Let's go through the reasons of these accidents...

DOG HYGIENE

First of all, it is important to highlight that dogs are clean animals.

Ever since their childhood, they naturally go away to do their business. Therefore a puppy is clean from the very first weeks of his life.

Be sure to keep in mind that dogs do not naturally go outside to do their business. To achieve that, you will have to make them understand that peeing in the house is forbidden. The best way to train a puppy is to congratulate him every time he urinates outside the house.

WHY DOES MY DOG URINATE IN THE HOUSE?

It can happen that a dog urinates indoor, even though he was perfectly clean before. The causes can be of two sorts:

- **Physiological causes**: the dog may have a urinary infection that prevents him from holding in long enough to go outside. If your dog suddenly starts urinating in the house, it is essential that you take him to a vet.
- **Behavioral causes**: peeing in the house is very often due to the dog's behavior. Your dog may be too fearful to go out

to do his business or he may be too nervous every time you leave the house.

If this indoor urinating lasts, you may need the help of a specialist such as a vet or a dog behaviorist.

MY DOG PEES AT NIGHT: WHAT SHALL I DO?

Sometimes, a dog urinates inside the house only on specific moments, for example at night.

This might be because your pet can not hold in overnight. If he is still a puppy, don't worry: it takes a few weeks for a dog's bladder to be strong enough to hold in for hours.

Otherwise, your dog may have contracted cystitis and you should take him to the vet.

In any case, make sure to take your dog for a walk every morning and every evening so he has time to do his business before you go to bed and as soon as you wake up. Knowing that he will go out for a walk in the morning will help your dog hold in overnight.

TRAPS TO AVOID

The worst mistake when a dog urinates inside your house is to punish him! Unless you catch him red handed, he will never understand why you are yelling at him. And forcing his nose to his feces will confuse him all the more.

Isolate your dog when cleaning his mistakes. And remember to always congratulate him when he relieves himself outdoor.

You should also avoid training your dog to pee on a newspaper. It is a bad habit as it confuses your dog between newspaper and carpet. Therefore, it is much better to immediately train him to urinate outside, even if it implies cleaning stains at the beginning.

TEACHING NOT TO BARK

A barking dog can quickly become irritating, especially when he barks at night… or all day long! You will need to find a solution to this situation. Let's see how you can silence a barking dog.

UNDERSTANDING DOG BARKING

First of all, let's remember that it is absolutely natural for a dog to bark as it is his means of communication. Nevertheless, if your dog keeps on barking all the time, he has a problem. Apart from annoying and irritating you and your neighbors, he is also trying to show that there is something wrong.

Barking is the expression of several feelings:

- Protection of the household
- Fear
- Boredom
- Frustration

As you can see, barking is the way dogs express anything and everything. They sometimes even bark only to get your attention. How to avoid this annoying behavior?

MY DOG NEVER STOPS BARKING: WHAT SHOULD I DO?

The very first solution is training! Before thinking about buying an anti-barking collar or other tools, it is better to understand why a dog barks and to train him. Thereby you can limit the behaviors that trigger his barking.

In order to do so, here are some tricks to use when teaching him not to bark:

INITIATE THE DOG TO OTHERS AND TO EVERYDAY LIFE SITUATIONS

The two main reasons why a dog barks are fear and protective instinct. If your dog has never seen anyone else than you in his territory (that is to say in your house) he will naturally tend to bark at any noise or any newcomer entering the house. From the earliest days, invite people over and have your dog get familiar to the presence of other people. Also initiate him to everyday life situations (noise, traffic, crowd...) so he does not develop any phobia or a fearful character.

EXERCISING

A dog can also be barking because he is cruelly bored. If your pet seems to be very active, is damaging your home or your garden, the fault may not be his. If you neglect the everyday walk or sport, it may backfire on you in the form of loud barking and irritation!

DECIDING ON GAMES AND WALKS

Barking can also be a way to ask for your attention. If you pander to his every whim you will encourage him to bark more and more often. When you dog starts barking, ignore him or take him to another room: from the earliest days he has to understand that you are the one deciding when to go out for a walk or to play.

Caution: answering a dog bark by screaming will only excite him more and will reverse the effect you wanted.

Knowing how to ignore your dog: in order to stop your dog from barking when you are away, avoid being too enthusiastic every time you enter or leave the house. Never say goodbye to your dog when you leave: it will tend to make your dog bark until you come back.

TRAINING MY DOG NOT TO BARK

Fear, excitement, solitude or looking for your attention: whenever a dog starts barking he is never the first to get tired of it.

Paradoxically, training your dog not to bark will start with teaching him to bark to order, following these steps:

1. When he spontaneously starts barking, tell him to "bark". Wait for a few seconds and give him a treat. Repeat several times.

2. From time to time, tell him to bark: if he barks, give him the treat he deserves.

3. It is now time to introduce the "quiet" command. It should sound like this: "bark", the dog barks so he gets a treat, then "quiet" and if the dog stops barking, you give him another treat.

Then, you will have taught your dog to stop barking even when you did not cause the barking. Make sure you keep on rewarding him for a while every time he obeys the "quiet" command.

TRAPS TO AVOID

As always when training a dog, coherence will be your best ally. You have to have your dog understand the "quiet" command. It will be no use yelling at him: it would make him keep on barking and will set a limit to your voice raising possibilities. On the contrary, a very low "quiet" command will force your dog to concentrate on your voice and leaves you the possibility to raise your voice later.

Let's see the techniques to be completely avoided…

When your dog starts barking or, even better, when you feel he is on the edge of barking, you command him to be quiet and then:

- ○ You hit him: it unwinds but it is useless, violent, unfair (he did not kill anybody!), counterproductive and even

borderline in the eyes of animal protection. Let's just forget it.
- ○ You offer him a rewarding treat. If he stops barking, he gets the treat. That will make him bark more to get treat. To be avoided.
- ○ You throw an object at him (a toy for instance) to interrupt his thoughts and distract him from the reason why he is barking. This technique is useful but may, on the long run, cause a conditioning: "if I want you to play with me I bark for a while until you throw me a toy". Also to be avoided.

TEACHING NOT TO JUMP ON PEOPLE

A jumping puppy is anything but rare. Nevertheless, once the dog is grown up, it can quickly become dangerous… or just very annoying. This is the reason why it is very important to prevent a dog from jumping on people and to have him quit this kind of habits.

WHY DOES MY DOG JUMP ON PEOPLE?

First of all, let's remember the meaning of jumping. Dogs greet one another by licking or smelling their noses. Next time you see two dogs meeting, pay attention to them and you will notice it.

The problem is that a human's nose is out of their reach… unless they jump at your face. It can be very cute to see a puppy jumping at you but you will not feel the same once he is fully grown up. A dog can start jumping at anyone and become dangerous to the kids.

It is absolutely indispensable to train your dog properly so he understands that he should not greet humans the way he greets dogs.

HOW TO AVOID JUMPS?

Fortunately, there is a training technique that will help you avoid this bad behavior. As usual, it will require a toy or a treat.

If your dog greets you excitedly when you arrive and is about to jump at you, go back behind the door and leave it ajar to see your dog. Then, show him a treat or a toy to get his attention.

Once he has seen his reward, give him the "sit" command. Obviously, you will have to train him to sit on command first. After he has been sitting long enough, come in and reward him.

After some time, substitute a toy for the candy. If all the members of the family follow this rule, your dog will eventually quietly wait for you.

It is essential to repeat this training very often and to use it when you have guests. Otherwise, your dog will not understand that he must not jump at other people either.

TRAPS TO AVOID

Finally, here are some BAD ways to be avoided if you want your dog to stop jumping at people:

- **Yelling at the dog**: a jumping dog is excited to see you. Yelling at him or getting angry will only excite him more which is exactly the reaction you do not want. Always keep calm when your dog jumps at you!
- **Rejecting the dog**: the dog jumps at people to get attention. Rejecting him would be a terrible mistake. Just ignore him, without touching him or looking at him. The best is to cross your arms and turn your back at him while commanding him to sit.
- **Enthusiastically greeting your dog**: it would encourage his bad behavior. Act calmly so that each of your passages does not become an event he should celebrate!

LEARNING TO GO TO HIS BASKET

The "go to bed" or "go to your place" command is very useful if you want your dog to stay calm. To train your dog to obeying this command, you need to follow a very precise technique. As always when it comes to dog training, this trick requires a lot of patience and involvement.

WHAT IS IT FOR?

It consists in training your dog to go back to his place (his basket, his favorite cushion, a specific room in the house, etc.).

Imagine you are having guests for dinner and your pet starts going mad and annoying you. Wouldn't it be useful to have him quietly go to his basket (cushion, room, etc.) just by telling him to?

INITIATING A DOG INTO HIS BASKET

To make the exercise work, it is better to use a basket your dog already knows and likes. The "go to your place" is to be taught when the dog is already several months old and preferably after more basic commands ("stay", "lie down", etc.).

CHOOSING THE LOCATION

First of all, the basket or cushion has to be properly located. The best is to place it in a calm and safe place, away from the coming and going.

Leave the basket in a spot where the dog feels comfortable but avoid its being in the middle of the way (hall, stairs, etc.)

INTRODUCING THE BASKET TO YOUR DOG

If you are training a puppy, the best for him is to understand what his basket is for and where it is located.

It is important for the dog to consider the basket as a resting place. It should not be associated to punishment or, even worse, to detention.

Never force your dog into his basket nor to staying in it.

TRAINING YOUR DOG TO GO BACK TO HIS PLACE

Training a dog requires a lot of patience and specific techniques. Here are advices to train your dog without rushing him.

You only need to follow these steps:

1) LURE THE DOG TO THE BASKET

To start with the actual puppy training method, take a dog candy.

Show it to your dog without giving it to him. Then, using the treat, have him go to his basket. If you choose the proper treat, there should be no problem for your dog to follow you... licking his lips!

Once the dog is in his basket, give him the treat and step aside. Try to have him stay in the basket without rushing him. Repeat the exercise several times.

You can encourage him to stay by playing with him or stroking him.

2) LEARNING THE "GO TO YOUR PLACE" COMMAND

As always, training your dog to obey this command is a matter of repetition. When the dog starts to understand that you want him to stay in his basket, use the command you want him to associate to the gesture ("go to your place", "go to your basket", "basket", or else).

The aim is for the dog to associate this command to *being in* his basket.

Keep on rewarding him by giving him treats or strokes when he stays in his basket. Practice several times a day but make sure you do not spend more than half an hour per day on the same exercise if you do not want your dog to get bored.

3) INTENSIFY THE EXERCISE

Gradually step back a little more every time. The dog should rush to his basket as soon as he hears the command.

If he does not obey at first, get close to the basket and repeat the order. You may need to lure him again until he understands what you expect from him. Try to gradually step away from the basket and always wait a little longer before rewarding him.

Never pull your dog by the collar or push him into his basket. For the training to be successful, it has to be a choice *he* makes.

Important: after a while, stop giving him treats and just congratulate him. The most important is to make sure you always reward him and show him your satisfaction when he obeys the command.

LEARNING TO STAY HOME ALONE

During the first days he spends in your home, the puppy is the center of everybody's tenderness and attention. Even though you feel like pampering him, it is the ideal moment to start training him to stay home alone. To avoid your absence being a painful moment for him and your coming back a painful moment for you, you should start practicing soon! Here are some tricks to make this training easy.

TRAPS TO AVOID

Many mistakes are due to the first days bonding, to the owners' too good intentions and to their lack of motivation faced to difficulty.

Remember you are doing this for his own good... and yours.

A dog who has not been trained to being alone will spend the whole time of your absence barking and howling, which will irritate your neighbors. He may also dirty or destroy your home which can be very trying to you and damage your relationship.

Don't wait: when your dog first enters your home, he is so adorable that you cannot think of anything else than spending time with him, playing and pampering him. This is a blessed time for him and it helps him get over being taken away from his mother. If you postpone his training to loneliness too much, it will be a real trauma to see you leave.

Do not transform your departure into a ritual: if you fill up his bowl, put on your shoes and look for your keys just before going out, he will associate all these actions to your upcoming absence and he will start to feel terribly and desperately nervous. All your stuff should be close to the door and easy to grab.

Do not grant importance to your departure: if you cuddle him, kiss him or talk to him just before leaving, you create a strong emotion followed by a great desillusion. These gestures reveal your own anxiety about leaving him, which is highly contagious. If tenderness equals stress, you are going to trouble him on the long-term. Do not feel anxious or, at least, do not let him feel your emotions.

- Do not leave secretly: it is counter-productive; your dog will feel cheated and disappointed.
- Make sure you close all the windows.
- Do not lock him up in a room. It is a short-term solution that will have negative consequences on the long-term.

GESTURES AND BEHAVIOR TO TRAIN YOUR DOG TO STAYING HOME ALONE

To make your absence a peaceful moment for your dog, he should be aware that you are going out but not give it much importance.

- Get him used to short absences from the very first days. Leave for 5 minutes then 10, etc. Once he understands that you come back every time even when you have been away for long, he will feel reassured. Do not follow a strict timing: he should not associate a specific hour with your absence.
- It is better for him to see you leave. Hiding your departure is useless.
- Ignore him 15 minutes before leaving and 15 minutes after you are back home to help making it a non-event and avoid creating desillusion or stress or excitement.
- Make sure he will not need to do his business when you are away. Take him out for a walk half an hour before leaving.

- ○ If you have neighbors, tell them you just adopted a dog and he might be a little noisy at first.
- ○ Make sure there is nothing dangerous or unstable around (knives, wires).

SOCIALIZING YOUR DOG

Let's hear what Mouss The Dog has to tell us about his socialization:

"When I was younger, I was not the mature and well educated dog I am now. I had never seen a cat nor heard the thunder and even in my worst nightmares I could not have imagined our neighbor's boisterous children! Fortunately, my parents knew that socializing a dog is very important to forge his future behavior. It should be integral part of his training."

KEY LEARNING TO SOCIALIZATION

"Socializing your dog means exposing him to many situations and different environments in order to make him be more courageous and as nice as possible towards strangers and other animals. Of course, it requires a lot of efforts before it bears fruits. In collaboration with Cats and Dogs, here are some examples of activities that will allow your dog to become a model dog like me."

NOISES:

Mouss: "The first time you hear thunder you feel like the sky is about to fall on your head. You will not be surprised if I tell you that it is not pleasant either to have people yelling close to you. Fortunately I have been taught very early that I should not be scared by surrounding noises. Cars would also have frightened me if I had not had the chance to walk busy streets since the age of 3 or 4 months."

CAR TRAVELLING:

Mouss: "One of my friends went on holidays with his owners when he was three... it was his first time in a car! I still remember how traumatizing this moment was for him. Fortunately, I have regularly been travelling by car since I was young. It is much easier to fight against your frights when you are still a puppy."

STRANGERS AND MANIPULATION :

Mouss: "Some dog breeds hate being stroked: it is in their genes. The capacity to accept people's affection also comes with socialization. Being manipulated by everybody since his puppyhood will train your dog to liking strokes – or to endure them – and to be less aggressive when strangers insist on playing with him.

On a similar note, I would never have accepted having my nails cut, being stroked on the legs or having my teeth brushed had I not been used to it since I was a puppy. It is now part of my daily routine."

CHILDREN:

Mouss: "Not all the children are good at playing with us! Being pushed and pulled around is never enjoyable but I learned to be more tolerant when I met Paulo, the neighbors' son... What a shock it was when he first tried to climb on my back. Fortunately, his mother was there to look after him and temper his energy. I now know that kids have trouble channeling their strength... but still, I sometimes prefer hiding!"

OTHER ANIMALS:

Mouss: "Even though I do not really like cats, I think it would have been worse if I had not cohabitated during two years with my owners' old cat. If you want your dog to be prepared to such a situation, why not make a deal with a friend to have your dog and his cat spend some time together? Same thing with other dogs: the dog park is like kindergarten for children: it teaches them to cohabite."

If you manage to master these learning processes, it will be a great start!

WHEN TO START SOCIALIZING A DOG?

If you wait for too long, your furry friend may develop bad habits that will be difficult to correct.

Also, the breeder has a decisive role to play: he should start between the 4th and the 8th week. The dog should not be separated too early from his mother but it is important to start his socialization when he is young, even if only by stroking and introducing him to slightly stressful noises.

TEACHING TRICKS

TRAINING TO BRING BACK

Training your dog to fetch and bring back an item is one of the most basic training technics because it is a very common dog game. Is there anybody who can say he never tried throwing a ball to a dog saying "Fetch"? But this trick requires a good technic. Here are all the secrets to master this trick.

TEACHING YOUR DOG TO BRING SOMETHING BACK TO YOU

As for any dog training technic, this one requires a lot of patience and energy. Do not expect to train a dog in a couple of hours!

To train your dog to do this trick, you will need to carefully follow the steps explained in this article. As always, systematically favor positive reinforcement. If you want your dog to learn well and fast, you should never use punishment but only rewards!

1. CHOOSING THE PROPER ITEM

First of all, you need to choose the toy you will use. It is better to choose a wide and colorful toy that your dog will easily spot.

Avoid tennis balls or toys that are not specifically made for dogs (especially hard objects): they may damage your dog's teeth or give him stomach ache.

2. FINDING THE PLACE TO TRAIN

As usual when training a puppy, you will need to start in a quiet place because a young dog has trouble focusing. If he is surrounded by people or noises, he will not learn anything.

Start in a quiet place your dog already knows, like your garden or a nearby public park.

If your puppy is really young, choose a closed place so he cannot run away.

3. LEARNING TO BRING BACK

If you have already started training your puppy, you know it requires repeating many times the same gestures. Training to bring back is no different.

Start with choosing a command, that is to say a sentence to pronounce when you want your dog to bring the object back. It can be the classical "Fetch". To make it more efficient you can add a gesture to this command, like miming throwing an object away.

Then, you only need to throw the toy while repeating the command and the gesture. If your dog does not react, go get the object by yourself, then calmly go back to your initial position and repeat the movement.

Once your dog has taken the object, stay still and wait for him to bring it back to you. Make sure you congratulate him every time he brings it back by giving him a dog candy. Then, little by little, substitute strokes for candies.

4. LEARNING TO DROP

One of the most difficult steps will be to teach him to drop the object. Keeping their toys in their mouth is part of dogs' domination logic. They want to prove they are the strongest by refusing to give anything away.

As you already figured, training to give will require his loosing this habit. The worse thing to do would be to start a physical fight with your dog. You should absolutely avoid playing the hero because it might force your dog to keep the object longer.

Training to give is the same technic as the previous one, associating a command and a gesture. You can for instance say

"Drop" or "Give" while showing the palm of your hand. If your dog does not react, slightly pull the toy and show your hand again. Once he has understood and dropped the toy in your hand, give him a treat.

This positive reinforcement technic will slowly make him give you the ball on command, without having to insist. It will require patience at first, just like all the other tricks you need for your dog to be perfectly well trained.

5. MOVING THINGS UP A GEAR

When your dog has mastered bringing back a toy on command in your garden, you can take him to a noisier place like a park or a forest.

Beware: do not leave your dog off the leash in a public place if he has not yet been trained to come back and walk to heels.

Once this trick is perfectly secured, playing ball with your dog will be a real pleasure in any situation.

TRAINING TO BOW

Who said only humans can be polite? Dogs can as well: they know how to bow. At least if their owners teach them the trick. If you wish to train your dog to bow, here is the method.

A NATURAL POSITION

For humans, bowing is a way of greeting someone whereas for dogs, it is a way of showing they want to play. This position looks like this: the dog has his two forelegs stretched on the ground and his bottom up.

If your puppy is playful, you probably already saw him bowing. But with a little patience, you can have him bow on command.

Let's see how to proceed.

THE METHOD

This trick is to be avoided with puppies before one year old as it might induce growth problems.

As for any other trick, it will require patience and work. Here are the steps you will need to take:

1. PREPARE THE POSITION

First of all, make sure you have some treats and candies around.

- Sit on the ground.
- Take a candy in your hand so your dog focuses on it.
- Then, stretch one of your legs and place your hand holding the candy under this leg. The idea is to have your dog squat to reach the candy.
- When he tries to catch it, give him a command ("Bow", or else).

2. HAVE THE DOG BOW

When trying to get the treat, your dog may naturally end up bowing. In that case, repeat the command you chose, congratulate him and give him the treat.

If your dog tries to lie down, put your second hand under his stomach to force him to stretch his back legs. Congratulate him when he gets back on his legs and give him the candy.

Repeat this exercise until he stops trying to lie down.

3. KEEP ON PRACTISING

Your dog will eventually bow naturally when he tries to fetch the treat under your leg. Little by little, you can raise your stretched leg so that the obstacle gets more difficult for your dog to by-pass.

Make sure you keep on repeating the command and on congratulating the dog when he bows.

The final aim is to stop using your leg as an obstacle when you want to make your dog bow. When he manages to bow upon request, make sure you keep on congratulating and rewarding him.

4. MASTER THE TRAINING TO BOW

To have the command perfectly mastered, you will need to repeat this exercise many times. There is no need to bore your dog with this exercise during hours: practice twenty minutes per day maximum and wait for the results.

The major advantage of this method is that you can easily use it at home.

Once your dog has perfectly understood the command, stop giving him candies but keep on congratulating and stroking him every time he obeys.

THE NATURAL METHOD TO TRAIN A DOG TO BOW

If you are interested in this trick but do not feel like having your dog practice specific exercises to bow, just wait for your dog to naturally bow. Every time he does, congratulate him and give him a treat. You will also need to associate a command with it so that he easily makes the connection between the treat and the bow. However, this method requires more time than the previous one.

LEARNING TO SAY "HELLO"

Dogs need to learn new things all through their lives to remain sharp and be at their upmost. Saying "Hello" and "Goodbye" is a basic trick people will love. Let's see how to teach it.

PREREQUISITE

There is no use in saying that your dog will not actually pronounce the words "hello" or "goodbye" but that he will express it in his own way. The leg is ideal for that purpose. So, first of all, your dog needs to be able to raise his leg on demand with the commands "Give your leg" or "Shake hands".

You are going to train him to wave his leg and to answer new words, and that is going to develop new qualities. To make sure he does not develop only leg dexterity, do not hesitate to force him to alternate the use of both legs.

THE STEPS

- Start the training with something your dog already knows well: the treat! As usual, it is better to have him understand right away that there will be rewards.
- Ask your dog to sit. Stand or sit in front of him, in the same position you use to shake hands with him. The treat is in your left hand while you wave at him with your right hand, as if you were going to shake hands with him.
- When he raises his leg, wave your hand and say "Leg, say hello" or any other command you want him to associate with this gesture. At the same time, you can give him his first reward.
- This step needs to be repeated many times until you consider it has been perfectly understood. Then, you can

gradually stop saying "Leg" at the beginning of the command.
- ○ Keep on waving your hand in front of him while saying "Say hello" or "Say goodbye". He has to be able to react identically to any of those two sentences.

The goal is to have your dog raise his leg and wave it every time he hears "Say hello" or "say goodbye".

TRICKS AND TIPS

To teach a new trick to your dog, you need him to be focused. For instance, a moment of excitement while playing is not a suitable time.

To keep your dog focused, treats, strokes and congratulations are way more efficient than punishment. Everybody agrees to use positive reinforcement nowadays.

Keep in mind that a step has to be perfectly understood before you can move on to the next one. And then you should not go back to a previous step except – and only – if it has not been clearly understood.

Also, do not hesitate to take a short break between two steps, especially if your dog's concentration breaks.

GIVING A KISS

Learning new tricks stimulates your dog's brain. The more a dog learns the more he can learn. It is both a game and a challenge to him. You have taught him all the basic tricks and are looking for a new one? Train him to give a kiss: this quiet and friendly trick will seduce all your friends!

STARTING FROM A NATURAL SITUATION

Not every dog is able to learn every trick. This one gives better results with an affectionate and trustful dog towards you and your family and friends. Indeed, some dogs will spontaneously put their nose on your cheek to show their kindness, in a natural rush of emotion.

First of all, you need to wait for your dog to give you a kiss. When he does, tell him to "Give a kiss", and then give him a treat or pet him.

The aim is to set his attention on this action.

Repeat the experiment several times, exactly the same way. The amount of times depends on each dog: some understand the trick after 5 times; others need to repeat the exercise 10 times or more.

MAKING YOUR DOG RECOGNIZE THE "GIVE A KISS" COMMAND

After some time, you can tell your dog to "Give a kiss". If he comes to you and puts his nose on your cheek, reward him with a dog candy, strokes or encouraging words. The dog then understands he has reacted the proper way and it will encourage him to reproduce the same behavior in an identical situation.

This step has to be repeated several times as well, but only with you at first.

After some time, if you consider that your dog has properly understood the trick, you can stop giving him treats. But keep on petting and encouraging him because your affection means a lot to him.

Once you are sure he has mastered the "Give a kiss" command with you, you can start asking him to give a kiss to someone else. Start with the people he knows best, like your family members.

If your dog does not seem keen on giving a kiss to someone, do not insist more than a couple of times. Maybe he does not know the person enough. Wait for him to feel more comfortable and try it again with a candy.

ADVICES TO HELP YOUR DOG

If you realize your dog does not recognize the "Give a kiss" command when out of context, you need to start the process over again.

Maybe your dog did not understand the relation between the kiss and the treat. Wait for him to be hungry to provoke this situation. A dog with an empty stomach is always more motivated and focused on learning new tricks!

This command should be part of his daily habits before you ask him to kiss your friends, especially if he does not know them.

"TOUCH" TRAINING

You can be sure that you will never regret training your dog to do this easy and useful trick. The "Touch" command does not seem much but it is the necessary start to many other tricks. Moreover, it provides a new opportunity to spend time with your dog. Here is the technic:

WHY SHOUD YOU TOUCH TRAIN YOUR DOG?

Most of the dogs like learning new things all through their lives. It is their way of:

- Understanding human's world better;
- Improving their communication with their owner;
- Keeping on developing their intelligence.

The "Touch" command has several advantages. First of all, it is an easy trick to teach, which makes it gratifying for your dog and yourself. If you are a young owner, this trick will help both you and your dog develop self-confidence.

Also, this trick can help your dog surpass himself. By making him touch your hand or items in uncomfortable situations, you will help him gain self-confidence and feel reassured. If you plan on practicing sports with your dog, this will be a useful tool to have him surpass himself.

Finally, this trick is the necessary base to learning many more.

HOW TO TEACH THE "TOUCH" COMMAND?

You will need dog biscuits and treats to reward your dog. As often, it is better to start the training in a quiet place and to wait until the process is well understood before moving on to a less quiet place.

1ST STEP: THE HAND

- ○ Stand in front of your sitting dog and show him the treat in your hand.
- ○ Hold the biscuit between two fingers of your open hand, palm toward your dog.
- ○ Let your dog come and take the biscuit and, when he takes it, say "Yes".
- ○ Repeat 10 times before you start doing everything the same way with an empty hand. If he comes and touches it, say "Yes" and reward him with a treat given from your other hand. Practice 10 times at least before moving on.
- ○ Once your dog systematically comes to touch your hand with his nose whenever your show it to him, the first step is mastered!

2ND STEP: THE "TOUCH" COMMAND

From now on, you can have your dog practice this exercise 5 minutes a day during a week and increase the distance between your hand and his nose. When placing your hand in position, say "Touch". At the end of the week, you can stop using treats and turn it into a game.

USE OF THE "TOUCH"

Your dog has now understood the principle. It is your turn to find playful challenges that will be fun for both of you and will develop his understanding and his agility. Do not hesitate to put some obstacles on his way (not too difficult, though!) to have him practice his agility. When he manages to pass an obstacle to touch your hand, make sure you congratulate him with lots of strokes and sweet words to encourage him all the more.

TRAINING YOUR DOG TO "ROLL OVER"

Here comes some gym along with a new trick! This one is a two-in-one trick that will bring fun to your dog and yourself: the "Roll over" command. It is obviously not one of the basic tricks in dog training but it gives your dog the opportunity to spend time with you, which is essential! Here is the technic.

TECHNICS

As often, there are several possibilities to teach a new trick to your dog. The most important is to have him understand what you expect him to do, in a consistent and positive way. Do not forget that once you have started using a method, you cannot switch to another one in the middle of the training.

Whichever the method you choose, it will start with the "Lie down" command. Therefore, your dog needs to know this one first.

TRAINING WITH A TREAT

- Ask your dog to lie down.
- When he is lying down in front of you, draw his attention to a biscuit, hold it over his head and make it go from one ear to the other. To follow the biscuit, he will have to roll over.
- Once he has rolled for the first time, reward him to make sure he understands that he did what you expected.
- Start over around 10 times before introducing the command "Roll over" at the beginning of the exercise. Make sure you reward him every time he reacts properly.
- When this step is fully understood, draw your dog's attention to your empty hand (no treats). Do the same gesture above his head to guide him and say "Roll over".

When he does, give him the treat that was in your other hand.
- When he has perfectly understood the trick, you can stop giving him treats and make your gesture more flowing.
- Finally, try giving him the command "Roll over" without doing any gesture. There you are: your dog knows how to roll over!

TRAINING WITH EASY GESTURES

Depending on the dog's height and his understanding capacities, some methods are more effective than others. The appropriate one to your dog will be yours to identify.

WITH YOUR ARM ON HIS NECK

When the dog is lying down and his attention is set on you, put your fore-arm on his spine. With your other hand, catch the foreleg that lies next to your elbow and bring it nicely to the other side to make the dog turn around. Reward him with congratulations and a treat.

Here, the impetus is fully yours. Then, the dog will slowly start to make the movement along with you. While keeping your arm on his neck, slowly reduce the foreleg rotation and add the command "Roll over".

You can stop using your arm to guide the roll once he has perfectly understood the command.

GETTING HIM TO LAY ON HIS BACK

When the dog is lying down, hold a biscuit over his right ear and move it to his left back-leg or the other way round. It will force him to roll over. Repeat the command "Roll over" every time.

Start over until he has understood and slowly stop giving him a biscuit. The dog should eventually understand the gesture of your finger turning over his head.

LEARNING TO CRAWL

Looking for a fun trick? This one will help your dog be more flexible. Let's see how you can make him understand what you want from him with this step by step method.

GETTING READY

As often, there are prerequisites to this trick. To crawl, your dog needs to know a more basic trick: lying down on demand.

To help your dog understand what you expect him to do, let him see the treats he will get. It will help him focus on your movements and words.

This trick is easier for small breed dogs but large dogs can make a success of it as well. In case of a large breed dog, train him to crawl when he is young: his small size will help him do it easily. He will just need regular practice to keep on doing it all his life.

THE STEPS

There are 4 major steps for your dog to crawl:

REMAINING FLAT ON HIS STOMACH TO CATCH A SWEET
- Stand a few centimeters away from your dog and tell him to lie down.
- Show him a candy and hold it in front of him. When he tries to catch it, slowly move your hand away from him.
- If he reaches your hand without standing, give him the treat and start over several times so he understands what you want him to do.
- If he stands, it may be because you removed your hand too fast. Slow down.

- All through the training, give him the candy when he is the lowest so he understands which position he has to maintain.

THE HAND GESTURE

Place an open hand in front of him, empty of candy, and move it away slowly to make him crawl in its direction. After he has crawled a few centimeters, you can give him a reward with your other hand and congratulate him.

Your movement has to be very slow: if you go too fast, he will immediately stand to follow your pace.

CRAWLING ON A BIGGER DISTANCE

Stand aside your lying dog and walk very slowly, at his pace. He should crawl at your side. Stop after a meter or two to reward him.

Repeat several times.

USING THE COMMAND "CRAWL"

When he starts moving, give him the command "Crawl" so he associates the word with the action. This step also has to be repeated several times. Every time he understands and obeys, congratulate him with nice words and pet him.

ADVICES TO MAKE YOUR DOG CRAWL

Before you start the exercise, make sure the floor is not slippery. Tiles or a marble floor may be a problem and induce the need of a carpet to help the dog crawl properly.

Make sure you regularly encourage and stimulate your dog when he reacts as expected but do not punish him when he fails. Both of you will need patience to get what you want!

WALKING BACKWARDS

Having your dog walk backwards is possible and can prove very useful if he ever becomes too invading or when playing dog sports. Let's see all the tips about this trick.

WHY WOULD A DOG WALK BACKWARDS?

This command is as fun a trick as the "Sit", "Lie down" or the "Shake hands" commands. And the good news is that dogs usually learn it fast!

You will find several reasons to train your dog to walk backwards:

- It keeps the dog out of your territory.
- It can be useful if the dog gets annoying or insistent, especially when you are welcoming guests.
- It is a very basic gesture that is often used when practicing heelwork to music.

USE A CLICKER

The following method is based on positive reinforcement and requires the use of a clicker.

You will need:

- **Dog candies**: the candy is the reward you will give to your dog to congratulate him on his good behavior. It will encourage him to learn faster.
- **The clicker**: this small plastic box emits a double 'click' sound when compressed. It is used to reward a specific behavior and works on your dog's willingness to please you and earn his prize.

You will easily find clickers in pet shops or on specific websites.

Good to know: clicker training can be used for any trick you want your dog to learn!

THE METHOD

There is nothing easier than training your dog to walk backwards. Just make sure you have patience and follow these steps:

1. REARRANGING SPACE

First of all, you need to rearrange the room to create a corridor behind your dog in order to force him to walk back in a straight line.

This corridor can be made of cardboard or chairs. Your dog should stand before two chairs or two obstacles between which he can easily walk. But the space between the two obstacles should be narrow enough to avoid your dog walking diagonally.

2. STARTING THE EXERCISE

- To start the training, place your dog between the two obstacles. You can use a reward to lure him into standing where you want to.
- Once he stands between the obstacles, stand in front of him, quite close, and wait for him to walk backwards. If he does not, step ahead to force him to step back.
- When he does, click and reward him before going back to your initial position. Congratulate and pet him as soon as he starts walking backwards.

3. TEACHING THE "WALK BACKWARDS" COMMAND

When your dog starts understanding the exercise, you can combine the clicker with a command.

Keep on rewarding your dog until he starts understanding the command and spontaneously walks backwards when asked to.

As for any other exercise, it requires a regular practice, without spending hours on it. If the dog is not enjoying the training and feels forced to practice, he will not learn properly.

4. INTENSIFYING THE EXERCISE

When your dog masters the "Walk backwards" command, you can remove the obstacles to keep on practicing. The aim is for your dog to walk backwards in a straight line even if nothing stands on his way.

Repeat as often as necessary until your dog understands the exercise perfectly.

Clickers and treats will eventually be useless. But make sure you keep on congratulating your dog to show him your satisfaction.

TURNING ON/OFF THE LIGHT

Learning is the best way to remain young and fit. If he could speak, your dog would tell you how much he loves learning new tricks and games every day. You have taught him the basics – "Sit", "Stay", "Go to bed", "Heel", etc. – and now you lack inspiration? Here is Mouss the Dog's idea: train your dog to turn on and off the lights!

PREREQUISITES

This trick is not for beginners. Indeed it requires precision and a dog that is used to training. Keep in mind that you should never drop training your dog if you want to obtain good results. That way, you stimulate his intelligence and help him understand his environment.

An intellectual activity such as sports is a good way for him to stay on top of his capacities.

TRAINING METHOD

The results are always better when a positive method is used: reward good behavior, ignore bad behavior and do not punish.

The clicker will be very useful to obtain a precise result on the long-term. Clicking every time your dog behaves the expected way will encourage him to take decisions while remaining attentive to your reaction, which is a constructive and motivating attitude. This technic really gives surprising results!

THE STEPS

This trick will take an hour, with a minimum of two breaks. If you feel your dog needs more time, you can practice several times but do not insist too much or he will be demotivated.

FOCUSING ON THE WALL

Stand next to your dog, close to the wall where the switch is. At that point, your dog totally ignores what you want him to focus on. He should not be looking at you. Encourage him to look away. Wait for some time. When his look happens to be on the wall, click and reward him. After a few times, he will understand that he has to focus on the wall.

SHOWING THE SWITCH

When the first step is secured, you can move on. Wait for his look to be more specifically set on the switch then click and reward him. From now on, only reward him when he looks at the switch.

He will quickly understand that the switch is the point of the training.

TOUCHING THE SWITCH

Stop rewarding your dog when he has perfectly identified the switch and wait for him to touch it with his nose or his paw. Start by clicking and rewarding him in both cases. When he has understood that touching is compulsory, only reward him when he touches the switch with his paw.

ASSOCIATING THE COMMAND

You can click and congratulate him when he turns the light on or off. If he touches the switch without result, ignore it.

It is only after the dog has made the connection between the reward and the change of light that you can add the word "Light" to his action.

Depending on the dog, each step can take longer. Be patient and make more breaks if you see that your dog gets tired or bored.

TRAINING TO RECOGNIZE ITEMS

You would be surprised to know how much information a dog can learn! For example, did you know that a dog can be trained to recognize the names of different items? If you have always dreamt of having your dog bring you your slippers and newspapers, you will love this trick.

CAN A DOG IDENTIFY THINGS?

Owners very scarcely take time to teach their dog words. However, dogs are perfectly capable of recognizing the names of several items.

For instance, there is a good chance that your dog knows what a "toy" and a "ball" are. He just needs training to recognize other objects and even bring them to you...

This trick has many uses:

- It is the first step to having him bring the item back.
- It stimulates the dog's intelligence.
- It improves his obedience.
- It reinforces the dog/master relationship.

HOW TO TRAIN HIM TO IDENTIFY ITEMS?

As usual when it comes to dog training, you will need patience to master this one.

Here is the ideal method to help your dog memorize several items' names:

1. INITIATE YOUR DOG TO SEVERAL ITEMS

As a start, you need to allow your dog to discover several items. The best is to start training with a unique item to make it easier: a ball, a toy, etc.

Ensure your dog perfectly knows the item. For instance, show him a ball, place it in front of him and say "Touch the ball" to make him touch it with his nose. During that step, always keep the item in your hand.

Practice a few minutes per day and make sure you repeat the name of the object several times to arouse your dog's curiosity.

After some time, switch the "Touch" command to the sole name of the object. When your dog touches the correct item, congratulate him, give him treats and pet him.

Use this method to have your dog recognize two or three items.

2. ENCOURAGE YOUR DOG TO FETCH THE ITEM

Once your dog know the names of one or more items, you can move on to the next level.

This time, do not keep the object in your hand but leave it somewhere close (on the ground or on a coffee table).

Name the item you want and check for your dog's reaction. If he touches or takes in his mouth the correct object, congratulate him.

Repeat this step once or twice a day, using all the objects your dog knows. You can repeat this step until your dog systematically has it right.

3. MIX THE ITEMS

After your dog has mastered this step, you can move on to the next one. This time, mix the items your dog knows to make sure he can identify them.

Put two of the known items on the ground (not too close from each other) while saying their names. The exercise consists in your dog touching the correct one when you name it.

Alternate the names and congratulate him whenever he touches the correct one. At first, to make it easier, you can show the object you name or even keep it in your hand.

4. MAKE IT MORE COMPLEX

You dog now identifies and recognizes several items? If you want, you can practice the same exercise with three or more objects.

With time you can try putting the items away to see if your dog goes get them. You can also associate the name of the item with the "Bring back" command to train him to give you the items.

Keep in mind that this exercise requires patience and time. Boring your dog during hours with the same exercise would be useless. It is much better to train him every day during a few minutes so he memorizes easily and enjoys it.

TRAINING TO PUT HIS TOYS AWAY

It is raining and your dog is bored? Why not train him to doing something new? Here is a trick that combines business with pleasure. If you are tired of putting his toys away after playing, here are some advices on how to train him to tidy up his stuff by himself.

PREREQUISITES

This trick is to be taught after easier ones. Indeed, to tidy up his toys, the dog needs sophisticated knowledge like knowing how to identify his toys from other objects in the room, take them in his mouth but not as a game, and drop them in the proper place.

To sum up, to put away his toys the dog needs to be able to recognize specific items and to obey the "Take", "Bring back" and "Drop" commands.

THE STEPS

This trick looks easy but it will require all the patience you have because some of the following steps might baffle your dog and take more time than you expected.

STEP 1: RECOGNIZING HIS TOYS AMONG OTHER ITEMS

First of all, your dog needs a place to play and a nearby toy box. You can start with teaching him the words "toy", "ball", "cord", etc. Avoid longer words (more than three syllables) when it comes to his stuff. At first, repeat the word when he catches the item and draw his attention to it. Then, pronounce the word and wait for his reaction. He should head for it.

STEP 2: MASTERING THE "TAKE" COMMAND

Wait for the dog to take an item and say "Take the ball", "Take the toy" while stroking and encouraging him. If he obeys, reward him with more strokes.

STEP 3: "BRING BACK", "GIVE", "TIDY UP"

Hold your hand above the toy box and ask him to "Give" or "Bring back" the scattered toys. If you realize he has understood, take your hand away and show him the box.

It is only after he has mastered this step that you can teach him the "Put your toys away" command (or the easier "Tidy up") by showing him the toy box and rewarding him when he reacts properly.

MORE ADVICES

During steps 1 and 2, it is recommended to reward the dog with strokes and encouragement so he does not drop the item he is holding in his mouth. During step 3, you can give him treats.

In the third step, the dog should drop his toy in the hand. This action may be stressful to dogs who fear their toy would be stolen away. It is very important to reassure him and spend a lot of time on this step.

Every time you realize the new step has not been understood, move back to the previous one and strengthen your dog's understanding: that will help him overcome the problematic step.

TRAINING TO OPEN AND CLOSE DOORS

Not everyone is interesting in this trick but it can be very fun. Let's see how your dog can open doors!

BEWARE

This is a double-edged trick. It can be very useful to train your dog to open doors but it also means giving him all the keys to doing what is forbidden. For example, if you store his food in a cupboard he can reach, there are chances he will eat it all when you are away.

Think it through and make sure you do not mind your dog opening doors before you start training him.

TRAINING YOUR DOG TO OPEN DOORS

You need a dish towel you are ready to sacrifice, a clicker and dog candies.

Follow the steps carefully, one by one:

1. PLAYING WITH THE DISH TOWEL

The towel is the main prop here. First of all, let your dog play with the dish towel. Encourage him to play with it as it if were a toy and show him how interesting this fabric is!

2. TYING IT TO A DOOR HANDLE

Now that your dog is having fun with the dish towel, tie it to a cupboard or a drawer handle. Make sure it is not too high for your dog to reach.

Your dog should remain interested in the towel. Remember to congratulate him with the clicker or treats every time he gets close to the towel.

Your role is to encourage your dog to take the dish towel in his mouth. Congratulate him only when he does, even if only for a second.

If you do not have a clicker you can use a whistle to congratulate your dog

3. LEARNING TO OPEN DOORS

Let's now make the exercise more difficult by rewarding your dog only when the cupboard door or the drawer moves. This way, your dog will slowly understand he has to pull the towel.

Combine this exercise with a command (for instance "Open the door") and keep on congratulating him every time he makes the door move.

Congratulate your dog a little less every time. In the end, you should congratulate him only when he actually opens the door or the drawer.

4. GETTING COMPLICATED

When the dog really masters the exercise, you can try it with other doors. To make it more complicated, try with higher or different types of doors.

Your dog may never be able to open a door with a knob. Mostly train him to open doors he can move with his paws.

TRAINING A DOG TO CLOSE A DOOR

This one is even more useful a trick! Indeed, you dog can close the doors you left open!

The technic slightly differs from the previous one.

1. PRACTICE WITH A DRAWER

The dish towel is not needed anymore. You only need to open a drawer. Start with a drawer your dog can reach. The ideal is to use the same drawer he trained to open.

This time, reward the dog with the clicker or a treat as soon as he touches the drawer with his paw. Reward him whenever the drawer moves and congratulate him all the more when he actually closes the drawer. Do not hesitate to combine this technic with a command ("Close the door" for instance").

When this exercise is mastered, use the same technic to train your dog on a higher drawer, to force him to stand on his back legs.

2. MOVING ON TO DOORS

When the drawer step is mastered, you can move on to doors. Use the same command for the door and the drawer.

Congratulate him the same way you did before: first when he touches the door, then only when the door is actually closed.

And... there you are! Your dog can now open and close doors!

TRAINING TO PLAY DEAD

Training a dog to learn tricks is a good way to work on his education and reinforce your relationship. Many masters enjoy the "Play dead" trick, very common when it comes to dog training. If you have always wanted to train your dog to play dead, take some notes!

WHAT TO WORK ON FIRST

Before trick training your pet, it is fundamental to teach him the most basic commands which are essential to his training, such as: "Sit", "Stand", "Lie down".

A dog who knows how to play dead is a dog that has been trained to stay still. Start with the basics before trying the following method.

HOW TO TRAIN YOUR DOG TO PLAY DEAD?

Once your dog has mastered the bases of dog training, you can train him to play dead. Theoretically, this trick can be taught to puppies before one year old. It can also be taught to an adult dog if he is already well trained.

Here are the steps to follow:

1) LYING ON THE SIDE

First of all, you need to train your dog to lie on his side.

To play dead he indeed needs to perfectly lie on his side. To that purpose, make him lie down then turn to his side with a treat. Squat down near the dog and show the candy to his mouth, then push him into going to the ground to get it.

Only give him the treat when his head is lying on the floor and he is on his side.

2) LEAVE HIM ON HIS SIDE

When your dog is on his side, command him not to move ("Stay still") to make him remain in this position. It is of course mandatory that your dog perfectly masters this command.

When he stays still, slowly stand up and try to have him remain in this position for a few seconds. Then congratulate him. At first, your dog will probably move as soon as you stand up.

Your first goal is to manage to reward your dog when he is on his side, not when he stands up. After some training, your dog will be able to remain still on his side for seconds before you reward him.

3) INTRODUCING THE "PLAY DEAD" COMMAND

When you realize your dog masters the exercise, you can introduce the related command.

Some people will say "Play dead", others "Bang". The choice is yours! The best is to combine a gesture with this command. The classical one is to point an imaginary gun at your dog.

Remember that you want your dog to associate this command with the treat. Keep on training him to do the exercise while reducing the quantity of treats your give him. Make sure you keep on congratulating and petting him.

4) GETTING HARDER

Keep on training your dog to play dead. It is compulsory that he perfectly understands the command and the gesture.

Eventually, you will not need to squat to make him lie on his side. The command should be obeyed even if you are standing. Also, you should train your dog to do this exercise not only when he is lying down but also when he is sitting.

Practice in different places so your dog does not only obey where he trained.

5) THE FINAL TOUCH

The "Play dead" trick consists in the dog lying down on his side, resting his head on the floor and staying still. During the first weeks of training, your dog will tend to wriggle once lying or not to rest his head on the floor. Also, he will need you to repeat many times the command to fully obey it.

Be careful about congratulating him when his head is on the floor. To push him into doing the whole exercise in one go, reward him more when he makes it perfectly, for example by giving him a bigger candy or more strokes and encouragement shouts.

This will make him understand he has to do it precisely and smoothly.

TRAINING TO SIT PRETTY

Is there any trick funnier than sitting pretty (also referred to as « Beg »)? This trick will be enjoyed by all your friends and family. Also, sitting pretty training is very fun and will reinforce your relationship to your dog.

ARE TRAINING AND GAMES THE SAME THING?

Training a dog first and foremost means having fun with him! The reason is that dogs learn better when they are playing and enjoying the moment. If you mix training with playing, you are on the right path!

This is why your dog can be trained to sit pretty through games.

HOW TO TRAIN YOUR DOG TO SIT PRETTY?

Training your dog is no hard thing... if you have a good method to follow and a lot of patience!

Here are the steps:

<u>1. FORCE HIM TO SIT UP STRAIGHT</u>
The dog can only practice to sit pretty when he sits. Therefore, start with the "Sit" command.

For this exercise, you need to be at the same height as your dog, so do not hesitate to squat next to him.

As always, you will need a treat to train him to do this trick. When your dog is sitting, hold the treat above his head: it will force him to sit on his back legs.

<u>2. TEACHING THE COMMAND</u>
When your dog "stands" (he must be on his hindquarters but raising his forelegs to try and catch the candy), give him the

command (it can be "Sit pretty" or "Beg") and give him his reward.

Make sure you congratulate him a lot in order to make him associate his behavior with the rewards.

You dog may not be able to hold the position at first. In this case, you can help him with your second hand to steady and reassure him. The first goal here is for him to stay seated on his back legs. At first, this unusual position may be uncomfortable for him. Help him with your free hand, and then take it away and congratulate him when he finds his balance, even if only for a few seconds.

3. REPEAT THE EXERCISE

This exercise has to be practiced every day. The more you repeat it, the more your dog successfully obeys. Of course, the best being the enemy of the good, there is no need to bother your dog with this training for hours every day.

At first, always hold a treat above his head to tempt him. After some time, try giving him the command "Sit pretty" without treats and finally try it even when your dog is not sitting.

As usual, never forget to pet and congratulate him as soon as he obeys. Repeat this exercise 3 to 5 times a day. After a few weeks of training, he should be able to sit pretty even without the promise of a treat.

TRAINING YOUR DOG TO STAND ON HIND LEGS

If the previous trick is not enough for you, why not train your dog to stand on hind legs?

This position is a "sit pretty" but with your dog standing on his back legs instead of being seated.

Obviously, your dog should first of all perfectly sit pretty before training to stand on his hind legs.

Training is simple:

- Command your dog to "sit pretty".
- When he does, hold a treat above his head.
- Encourage him to stand on his back legs to catch the treat.
- Give him the command you wish to associate with this position when he catches the treat and reward him.

Here also, your dog will need to train for a while, several times a day, before he perfectl

PLAYING WITH YOUR DOG

GAMES AND TRAINING

Playing does not mean wasting time. Especially for dogs! The reason is that training a dog goes through his ability to play. Games fully take part in puppies' training and in their growth. Let's clear this up.

THE BENEFITS OF GAMES

Dogs love playing with their owners for hours and it is essential to give them time and energy. Playing with your dog is a real benefit for him and neglecting him would make him miserable.

Here are the reasons why games are perfect for your dog:

- **The dog/owner bond**: First of all, playing with your dog will create a real complicity. Setting rules to the games you play with your puppy also teaches him to obey while having fun. It is a crucial step to make your dog learn what his place in your family is.
- **Awakening**: An educative game systematically helps your dog develop his competences. Playing makes him discover the world and learn new rules.
- **Exercise**: Dog games also play a big part in improving your dog's physical capacities. When fetching a ball or running, he exerts himself. Even better, fetching a stick or a ball develops his smell.
- **Dog training**: Playing with a dog is a way of educating him. To play, a dog needs to be well educated and trained. Training your dog the "Retrieve", "Drop the ball" or "Heel" commands will be necessary and educational games is of a great help.

TRAINING A PUPPY THROUGH GAME

Always keep in mind that training a dog will be much easier if you turn the exercises into games. As soon as he is a few weeks old, the puppy will try to find his place in your family. He will need landmarks to discover his new role.

Thanks to puppies' games, you will be quite capable of creating a strong relationship with your pet. Training games have strong social and educational effects on dogs. They will enable you to set strong bases for your pet training.

HOW MUCH TIME SHOULD BE GIVEN TO GAMES?

There is no need in saying that games will help your dog stay fit and healthy. Whether you go for a walk or use a dog toy, playing with him helps him train and also respect you. Let's see how much time a dog should spend playing.

DEPENDING ON THE AGE

Let's start with games that require specific precautions: a young dog has less stamina than an adult dog... keep that in mind!

To feel happy, a dog needs a maximum of 2 walks per day during half an hour. While you are at it, play with him but avoid making him run for more than 10 minutes and do not insist on practicing if he looks tired.

For a puppy, opt for specific toys that will not damage his teeth.

EXERCISES FOR AN ADULT DOG

A puppy quickly gets tired whereas and adult dog needs to play and practice a lot to exert himself. If your dog likes sports and games, take him out for a one hour walk minimum every day (you can make it two walks of 30 minutes). You can also choose to practice dog sports such as flyball, dog agility, etc. No doubt he will love them.

Playing with a dog is a good way of having him practice as much as he need. Throwing a ball or a dog Frisbee will encourage him to unwind and exert himself. But be reasonable: these games take a lot of energy. To avoid tiring your dog the best is to play games during 20 minutes max.

At home, you can keep on playing with him, for instance with a dog rope. But do not spend your whole time playing: to be a calm and well behaved dog, he also needs some quiet time alone. Moreover he needs to learn that playing or not is your decision.

Do not hesitate to buy him a dog chew toy like a Kong so he has fun on his own when you are away or do not feel like playing.

DANGEROUS TOYS FOR YOUR DOG

Do not forget that not every toy is safe. Many dog toys can prove dangerous. Therefore, letting your pet play with any toy involves risks. Here are all the advices you need to make sure you buy the proper toys for your dog.

DANGEROUS TOYS

Let's start with the toys sold in pet shops or on specialized websites: being sold as a specific pet item does not mean it is absolutely safe.

Here are the toys to avoid at any cost:

DOG BONES

Let's start with the old cliché. It is true that dogs really love chewing bones but they are dangerous for them. Even nylon bones sold in pet shops are dangerous.

That is because bones tend to spoil dogs' teeth, as well as any other too hard to chew toy. The worst of all are poultry bones which brake and may lead to intestinal perforation.

Absolutely avoid this kind of dog toys or dog candies.

OLD DOG TOYS

An old plastic toy presents a potential danger. A damaged toy may fall into small pieces your dog can have trouble digesting.

The consequences can be digestive problems or more severe complications. Conclusion: always throw away the old dog toys. And don't worry: your dog will be very happy to get a new one instead!

DOG TOYS COMPOSITION

It is also important to highlight the fact that some plastic dog toys include potentially dangerous substances:

- Phthalates
- Bisphenol

These products have been totally prohibited when it comes to children toys but can still be found in dog toys even though they can have harmful consequences on a dog's health.

To prevent these complications, make sure the toys you buy are free of phthalates and of bisphenol if they are made of plastic.

The Kong is a great example of a 100% safe toy!

OTHER DANGEROUS TOYS

Some owners let their dog play with toys that are not dedicated to them. Here is a list of toys you should avoid:

STAGS' ANTLERS:

They are no common dog game in Europe but our American and Canadian friends sometimes let their dog play with stags' antlers.

Although dogs like chewing antlers, these are very bad for them. They are too hard and there is a good chance that your dog's teeth will break. This is a NO!

In the same vein, avoid letting your dog chew wood sticks or anything too hard and harmful to his teeth.

TENNIS BALL

This one is another common mistake owners make: giving a tennis ball for their dog to play. This item is very bad for dogs.

Tennis balls are made of an abrasive material that will very quickly spoil the dog's teeth. Not mentioning how easy it is to tear it to pieces… and swallow them. Let's not take this bad habit and forget about giving a tennis ball to a dog.

Also avoid plastic balls, very easy for an animal to swallow. Better buy toys designed for large breed dogs because they are safe to chew.

CHOOSING A 100% SAFE TOY

The method to buy the perfectly safe toys your dog needs consists in studying the following criteria:

- **Size**: Do not let your dog play with something he may swallow. A dog toy should be larger than his mouth. Also avoid too big items as they might be too heavy and difficult for your dog to manage.
- **Small pieces**: Always choose a toy that cannot be dismantled. If the toy is made of small pieces, the dog might tear it apart and swallow them. To be avoided!
- **Solidity**: Avoid choosing a toy that is too hard or too strong. If you cannot twist or curve it with your hands, your dog will find it difficult to chew. It may even harm him.
- **Composition**: For all the reasons mentioned above, systematically prefer toys that are free of phthalates and bisphenol.

HOW TO CHOOSE THE PROPER TOYS?

Every dog likes playing games. They are very stimulating, especially for young puppies. When looking for a gift for your little ball of fur, choose a good one. Let's see how to be sure of your choice.

WHICH TOY TO CHOOSE?

Playing with your dog does not come down to buying him toys. Nevertheless, it is important that your dog enjoys playing with it. The reason is that they love chewing and playing with their toys. If you do not buy him toys, you can be sure he will play with a towel, a shoe or any other item of yours.

Dog toys are countless. The main guideline is to always choose a toy especially designed for animals and more specifically for dogs. Avoid tennis balls and other human games that may damage his teeth and even be toxic.

Among existing dog toys, we recommend:

DOG BALL

This one is the timeless standard. Basic and resistant, it is a safe bet if your dog likes to go fetch.

Even though it is a solid value, make sure you do not throw it too high: a dog may get hurt or twist his back while jumping. Also, prefer a dog ball to a tennis ball. Balls that are not specifically made for dogs can damage their teeth.

DOG FRISBEE

If you like throwing toys at your dog, you should definitely try dog Frisbee! Its main interest is to make your dog run and therefore practice sports, as the Frisbee is to be caught in flight. As for ball games, throw it at a reasonable height and as flat as possible so that your dog catches it without twisting his head.

Specific soft Frisbees for puppies are also available. Here as well, we recommend that you buy a specially designed for dogs Frisbee as they are more resistant than regular ones.

WOOD STICKS

In case you do not have any dog toy with you, make the most of the surrounding nature: dogs love wood sticks. Throwing one of those is a nice and fun game to play with your dog.

Be careful with the stick you choose: not every stick makes a good dog toy. Choose a simple stick, without branches or twigs that might hurt your dog. The stick should be resistant enough not to be eaten and light enough not to knock the dog out.

CHEW TOYS

Even if they love playing with you, dogs should also play on their own. A good option is to choose an educational toy the dog can play with when you are busy or away.

There are countless chew toys for dogs. Choose one that corresponds to the dog's size and that is not made of small dismountable pieces. Finally think before buying noisy toys: the noise can prove very stimulating for the dog… and very annoying to the owner.

KONG TOYS

These chew toys are also educative and can help you when training as they make a perfect reward for your dog. A Kong toy is made of plastic and can be filled with candies. As the dog will have to play with it to get the food, it is both a toy and a reward.

ROPE

If your dog does not like to fetch or if you are looking for an indoor game, rope is the perfect option. Like any other pulling toy, it will enable you to compare yourself to your dog. You pull on one side while he pulls on the other! It may look like a ratio of power exercise but it is a very fun one.

Nevertheless, you should teach your dog to drop the rope and calm down on command. Rope is more of a large breed and sportive dog game. Being a resistant and long-lasting item, whereas a ball or a Frisbee, your dog can play with it on his own without any risk.

DOG CUDDLY TOYS

Many are made especially for dogs. They will not damage their teeth and are very soft. But be careful: if your dog usually eats everything he sees the toy won't last long.

HOW MANY TOYS DOES A DOG NEED?

Do not spoil your dog! If you buy him too many toys, he will not know where to start... and may end up thinking any item he sees is a potential toy.

If you allow your dog to chew dozens of toys, you cannot expect him to understand that he cannot act the same with shoes, clothes and other human stuff he finds around the house.

Let him play with two or three toys at a time, alternating them. It will be more than enough for him to have fun.

HIDE-AND-SEEK

A lot of owners make playing games with their dog more complicated than it really is. It is not always necessary to buy connected or sophisticated dog toys. Sometimes, a basic hide-and-seek game is as fun and playful as anything else.

HOW TO PLAY HIDE-AND-SEEK WITH YOUR DOG?

This game may seem complicated at first but it is actually pretty easy to play with a dog. It is best played with a couple of players, plus the dog.

Here is how the game unfolds:

1. A family member will keep the dog busy while the other one goes hide. The best is to hide in a place where the dog cannot see you at all: behind the couch, under a bed or behind a door.
2. Once the person is hidden, the first one can release the dog. A command can be used, such as "Go find Daddy" depending on who's hiding.
3. If the dog does not find the hidden person, he can call him and repeat the dog's name every five seconds until he is found by the dog. That will prevent your dog from getting bored during the search. When the dog enters the room where the person is hidden, he should stop calling his name. If the dog still faces difficulties, the first person who stayed with him can point him in the right direction.
4. When the dog wins the game, meaning when he finds his target, the hidden person congratulates him with lots of strokes or a treat.

The more a dog plays hide-and-seek the better he gets. Over time, the whole family can play together to make the game greater.

You can also hide his favorite toy and make him look for it.

INVOLVING THE WHOLE FAMILY IN THE GAME

As you already know, a dog is a pack animal. To him, your family forms a real pack. It is no coincidence that a dog often obeys to the head of the family rather than the children. It only means he identified the head of his pack. Anyway, playing hide-and-seek is a great pack game for dogs.

It is an opportunity to involve your whole family in your dog training. Not mentioning that children also love this game!

Hide one at a time to play with your dog. Instead of asking him to "Find Daddy", say "Find Mum" or "Find Peter". Your dog will learn the family members' names at the same time.

INDOOR OR OUTDOOR?

At first, prefer indoor playing; remain inside the house. This way, your dog is not be disturbed by noises and it makes it easier for him to find the hidden person. These are important conditions for your dog to learn the game.

After some time you can try playing hide-and-seek in larger places like your garden and then a public park. Slowly increase the distance between the dog and the place where you hide to complicate the game.

Be careful not to let your dog off the leash in an open space especially if he has not been trained to obey the "Heel" command. A young puppy might get lost or run away if he finds himself alone in a big open space.

THE USE OF HIDE-AND-SEEK GAME FOR A DOG

If you think this is too childish a game, bear in mind that it has many advantages for your pet. For example and among others:

- ○ It develops his smell.
- ○ It trains him to find his owner easily.
- ○ It awakens his hunting instinct which is a strong stimulation.
- ○ It makes the "Heel" training easier as the dog will remember that finding his owner means getting a treat.
- ○ It strengthens the bond between the dog and his pack (his family).

In the end, hide-and-seek makes a great opportunity to have fun with your dog and train him at the same time. Why not give it try?

EDUCATING CHILDREN

A child attack is the obsessive fear of every dog owner, especially if they also have children. Yet, a nice dog is nothing unusual or unnatural. In many cases, when he gets bitten by a dog, the child is partly responsible for his injury, mainly because he had not been initiated to dog games. Let's see how to avoid such a tragedy to happen.

BEWARE OF THE DOG!

Even if your dog is the nicest of all, an attack on a child always is an eventuality.

Indeed, dogs' reactions as well as children's are difficult to predict. Therefore, you should be twice as careful when a dog and a child are playing together. It is important if the dog is yours and even more important if your child is playing with an unknown dog.

In any case, the best is to initiate your child to dog games to prevent a bite. Also, make sure you never let a young child and a dog unsupervised.

THE RULES TO OBEY

To limit the risks of a dog attacking a child, adopt basic safety rules. Here are advices regarding dog and child relationship that you need to follow:

- **Always watch the games**: For safety reasons, never let a dog and a child play unsupervised. Even if the dog is yours. It is the most basic rule to obey to prevent a bite.
- **Wait before you adopt a dog**: The majority if the children attacks are caused by recently adopted dogs and usually on children under 7 years old. If you do not have a dog and plan an adopting one, it might be better to wait until your

child is old enough to understand how to behave correctly with a pet.
- **Always talk with the dog's owner**: Your child wants to stroke a dog? First of all, ask for the owner's permission. This way, he can warn you if his dog does not like to be stroked or if he is aggressive. Generally speaking, never leave your child with an unknown dog.
- **Initiate your child**: As soon as your child is old enough to understand, talk about dogs with him, explain him how to behave when he is with a dog.

TEACHING A CHILD HOW TO PLAY WITH A DOG

Here are advices to share with your children before letting them play with a dog:

- **Keep calm**: Dogs consider yelling and abrupt gestures as forms of aggression. They are to be avoided, especially if the dog is not yours.
- **Be patient**: Just as humans do, dogs need time to get used to new persons. A child will have to take time to "introduce himself" to the dog. He will also be careful not to be too abrupt and wait before petting the dog.
- **Prevent attacks**: Children sometimes like hitting, pinching and even biting. Inform them that dogs hate all these and might fight back.
- **Leave a dog alone**: Your children need to learn not to disturb a sleeping or eating dog. Biting accidents often occur during one of those moments when the dog is on the lookout. Exactly like when the dog or puppy is playing with his own toys.
- **Staying away from his mouth**: Also recommend your children not to play with the dog's mouth. Getting close the teeth increases the risk of getting bitten.

If he keeps all these rules on his mind, your child will behave properly with dogs. This added to your constant supervision during games will reduce the risks of accidents. A healthy dog and child relationship brings a lot to both of them.

DOG SPORTS

INFORMATION ABOUT DOG AGILITY

Many owners look for demanding games that will enable their dog to spend his energy and improve his discipline at the same time. Dog agility fulfills this promise and even enables you to exert yourself too. But what is it exactly?

DISCOVERING AGILITY

You have never heard about dog agility before? It is a demanding and fun dog sport in which an owner directs his dog through an obstacle course.

The concept is simple: your dog runs through different obstacles, off leash and you can only guide him using your voice and running at his side as touching the dog is prohibited. In an agility competition, the race must be finished within in a precise time and time penalties are given whenever the dog makes a fault.

THE INTEREST OF AGILITY

This sport may seem complex at first but it presents several advantages for your dog and yourself:

- **The dog exerts himself:** Agility takes a lot of energy from your dog. This is why it is particularly good for dogs that live in small spaces or for a hyperactive dog that needs to expend energy.
- **The dog's discipline gets better**: Only a perfectly trained dog can achieve an agility course. Therefore, this sport can help you improve your dog's training.
- **Reinforcement of your relationship with your dog**: Agility is a team sport. It will therefore make your dog-owner relationship stronger.

REQUIRED EQUIPMENT FOR PRACTICE

If you wish to practice agility with your dog, there is minimum equipment required. Here are the things you need:

- **Obstacles**: Agility implies an agility field. The dog agility obstacles can usually be bought in dedicated agility clubs. The less expensive option is to find the obstacles on your own, especially if you are only starting the training.
- **An agility kit**: There are agility kits that include several obstacles you can use to create an agility course and practice in your own garden.
- **Dog candies**: To agility train your dog and make him like it, regular rewards are essential. Dog candies or biscuits will be perfect to that purpose.

WHERE TO PRACTICE?

The best way to discover this dog game is to enroll in a nearby dog agility club. It usually costs around a hundred euros for a one-year subscription. Belonging to a club is an opportunity to discover this game step by step and to meet other dog lovers.

Note that a minimum training is required before starting dog agility. You may need a professional dog trainer's help. That will not take any fun away from the training!

INFORMATION ABOUT FLYBALL

Flyball is a very unique game that makes your bond to your pet stronger.

WHAT IS IT?

Flyball is red-hot right now in the USA and in Canada where they even organize flyball tournaments!

This dog sport is a very interesting one. It basically consists in a four hurdles race to a box that releases a ball.

The rule is easy: Your dog goes on his own over this obstacle line at the end of which he triggers a flyball box pedal to release a ball he then catches on flight before going all the way back and giving you the ball.

It looks easy the first time you watch a flyball competition but be sure it requires a solid training.

ADVANTAGES OF FLYBALL

As many other dog games, flyball strengthens your relationship to your dog.

Moreover, this game highly stimulates him and boosts his training. Your dog will be more sociable, learn to come back to heels and to fetch an item, having fun and exerting himself all together.

One the main advantages of dog flyball, when compared to agility, is that the owner stays at the start/finish line instead of running at the dog's side. That means it can be practiced by elderly persons and persons with reduced mobility. On his side, the dog will need to be as energetic as possible.

WHERE TO PRACTICE?

Surprisingly – or not – France is a little late when it comes to flyball practice. Fortunately, this dog sport is getting pretty popular in France and finding a club should not be too difficult. Flyball tournaments have been organized since 2005 and are getting more common.

As often, the best option is to enroll in a flyball club in order to have all the required equipment and skilled people around. But before enrolling, your dog should already be well trained and in a good shape.

You can also buy a flyball harness and hurdles for a home practice but it will turn out to be more expensive and difficult.

INFORMATION ABOUT DOG SCOOTER

Here comes a more surprising dog sport: the dog scooter. This expression refers to a dog game you play with an off-road scooter. Beware: it is really challenging! Let's see how to practice this sport with your dog.

WHAT IS IT?

Don't worry if you have never heard of it before: as many other dog sports, it is not famous yet in France although it is very interesting and may become your new passion. Moreover, it makes change from basic dog games.

Originally imagined as a sled dogs' exercise, it is now an official dog sport.

HOW DOES IT WORK?

Dog scooter basically consists in a traction activity in which one or two dogs pull a scooter they are attached to by a special leash. Then, just let yourself be towed!

It is and ideal summer training for sled dogs. As for you, it is a great way to ride fast and enjoy the view without spending too much energy.

Before practicing this sport your dog must know how to pull a rope. Otherwise he will never get to understand the rules.

FOR WHICH DOGS IS IT SUITABLE?

As this game requires your dog to pull you, dog scooter is better reserved to stronger dogs. If you have a small breed dog, canicross will suit him more.

AND FOR WHICH HUMANS?!

You doubt you are up to dog scootering?

Don't worry: it is a pretty accessible sport because the one making the main effort is the dog. On your side, balance and flexibility are the main qualities you need.

Of course you also need to feel safe riding a scooter: being scared of falling or afraid of high speed won't help. The good news is: it is easier to jump off a scooter than off a bike. This is the reason why dog scooter is safer than canicross.

Before dog practicing, why not give a try to off-road scooter on your own to make sure you enjoy it?

EQUIPMENT

As any other dog sport, dog scooter induces the purchase of some material, at least:

- An off-road scooter
- A dog sport harness
- A specific leash
- Safety pads (for elbows, knees, …) and helmet

Do not overlook the pads (which are not for the dog but for you) and make sure you always wear them. They are indispensable to avoid severe accidents in the event of a fall.

A SAFE PRACTICE

Finally, let's go through some basic safety rules if you want to have a safe practice of this dog sport:

- **Go at your own pace**: Start practicing step by step. It is no use starting on a slope or an abrupt land. First try it in a park or on a flat ground. Then, move on to the next step.

- ○ **Go at the dog's pace**: Same here: respect your dog's needs. Do not practice for hours, especially if you notice your dog is tired.
- ○ **Beware of sickness**: Do not feed your dog just before or immediately after sports. It may induce stomach ache and nausea. The best is to stop feeding him three to four hours before exercising and waiting an hour after you finish.
- ○ **Avoid heat waves**: For your dog's good, do not practice dog scooter when the temperature is too high.

INFORMATION ABOUT DOG JUMPING

Finding a sport that suits your dog is crucial as he needs to spend energy to feel happy and be easy-going. Not mentioning that dog games enable you to assert your authority over your dog. If you are looking for a fun and demanding activity for your dog, think about dog jumping!

WHAT IS IT?

Jumping is a dog sport which focuses on the dog jumps through an obstacle race. This course usually includes slaloms, tunnels and obstacles, arranged to the owner's or the judge's wish.

Jumping competitions are organized and supervised by a jury and follow strict rules. The score depends on the dog's movements precision, the quality of the dog-owner couple, etc.

Competition is no obligation: you can simply enroll in a training club. It is a perfect way to strengthen your relationship with your dog. In case you discover a passion for this sport why not getting a license from an official training and agility commission so you can take part in competitions?

EQUIPMENT

You feel like giving it a try? First of all, you need to enroll in a dog agility club or a dog jumping club. Paying a usually very affordable annual fee will give you the chance to train and share experiences with other dog lovers.

If you wish to keep on training at home don't worry: there are many ways for you to create the perfect course by buying only a few items:

Dog obstacle: Many obstacles exist and can be used to create the perfect course

Dog tunnel: This one is a compulsory item. They are easy to find and store.

Dog slalom: Specific slalom courses are sold; they will help you train your dog.

PREREQUISITES

You dog will of course have to be well educated and trained beforehand. If he is not at your beck and call, the obstacle races will turn into nightmares.

Still, stay positive: many owners actually use dog sport as an excuse to keep on educating their dog and to work on their relationship and bond. Just initiate your dog step by step with the help of a dog trainer.

On top of making your dog exert himself, you will have a more peaceful relationship with him and will have less trouble making him obey your commands.

INFORMATION ABOUT CANICROSS

You are looking for a sport in which both your dog and you spend energy? Why not give a try to canicross? If you have never heard of it before, this article will tell you everything you need to know about this canine cross discipline and provide tips to help you find the best equipment to practice canicross.

WHAT IS IT?

Canicross, also named CaniX, is a sport in which a runner is attached to his dog. It is not exactly a Sunday morning jog with your dog. There are specific rules to obey:

- You have to run as fast as you can.
- You cannot overtake your dog.
- If your dog stops, you have to stop too.

Totally red-hot right now, canicross is an actual sport rather than just a game. Look for it and you will most certainly find canicross competitions organized by a real examination board.

THE EQUIPMENT YOU NEED

Canicross requires specific equipment. Here is a list of basic things you will need to start practicing:

- **A canicross harness**: to attach your dog to you without strangling him. It will of course be carefully chosen to match the dog's size.
- **A canicross leash**: a regular leash is not suitable for canicrossing. Buy a specific one that will be stronger and equipped with a shock absorber.
- **A canicross belt**: this is the human's version of the dog's harness! The canicross belt provides the runner with a

more comfortable experience as it maintains your lower back.

If you are interested in this sport, you may also be interested in canicross kits that include everything you need to practice.

WHERE TO PRACTICE?

Feeling like giving it a try? The best is to look for a nearby canicross club. It is the best way to participate in trainings and in actual races with other dog lovers.

As long as you have the needed equipment, canicross group training is not mandatory. There is no reason why you could not train on your own, with your dog. Especially as it is much recommended to train before the first race... if you do not want to fall from exhaustion before the finish line!

INFORMATION ABOUT HEELWORK TO MUSIC

If the above lines made you think "Heel-what to what?" you need help to discover what we are talking about here. This discipline is a mix of sport and obedience. It is getting more and more popular in France these days. Did this definition arouse your curiosity? Perfect! Now, let's look into it.

WHAT IS IT?

As for many other games, heelwork to music originates from England.

This technic derives from obedience training and looks like a dance in which the dog and his owner follow the music. Therefore the name! Since it has been approved by the Kennel Club in the United Kingdom and by the FCI (World Canine Organization, in English), it is now an official dog sport.

WHAT'S THE POINT?

Heelwork to music does not come down to dancing. There are more reasons to show interest in it:

- It is a game, meaning it helps you train your dog and have fun at the same time.
- It is a dog sport so it helps you share a demanding and fun activity with your dog while strengthening your relationship.
- If you are interested in both dance and dogs, heelwork to music is the perfect dog sport for you. It gives you the opportunity to choreograph a dance with your dog and even to perform in front of a public.

○ Heelwork to music is a perfect way for your dog to spend his energy and give the best of himself while you train him to obey.

WHERE TO TRAIN?

The best way to practice heelwork to music is to enroll in a club. This dog sport is available to any dog with a strong discipline and any owner with the required motivation to practice a lot.

Another option is to ask for a professional trainer's help who will help you train your dog through positive reinforcement. In any case, it is mandatory that your dog is perfectly trained before you get started.

TO CONTINUE...

We deeply hope that this book has inspired you and has helped you get close to your Golden Retriever.

Maintain and nurrish your relationship with your dog daily: there is no limit to the activities you can imagine to spend amazing moments together.

Now, keep this book and do not hesitate to look into it for inspiration when needed. Its ressources will always be available to reinforce your bonds with your Golden Retriever.

Do not put it away in a box: you might need it soon enough!

If you liked this book and want to help us promotize it, do not hesitate to write a nice comment on its Amazon product description.

Thank you for everything,

Mouss the Dog's Team

Published november 2018 - CARRE MOVA Édition

CPSIA information can be obtained
at www.ICGtesting.com
Printed in the USA
BVHW042208171218
535845BV00023B/1413/P